T0346640

APPLES OF GOLD

365 DEVOTIONS FOR LEADERS

BroadStreet
PUBLISHING

BroadStreet Publishing
Savage, Minnesota, USA

APPLES OF GOLD

© 2023 by BroadStreet Publishing®

9781424566877 (faux)
9781424566884 (e-book)

Devotional entries composed by Jared Winger.

Typesetting and design by Garborg Design Works | garborgdesign.com
Editorial services by Michelle Winger | literallyprecise.com

Printed in China.

23 24 25 26 27 28 29 7 6 5 4 3 2 1

He shepherded them
with a pure heart
and guided them
with his skillful hands.

Psalm 78:72 csb

Introduction

Being a good leader isn't easy. It requires courage, humility, integrity, and compassion. Jesus spoke of true leadership as having the ability to be a remarkable servant.

To be a successful leader, you must determine to follow the example of Christ no matter how difficult. There will be a cost. You may be scrutinized, wrongly accused, and pushed toward exhaustion, but take heart; there is a reward waiting for you if you do not give up. And it will be worth it.

Apples of Gold is a daily devotional for leaders like you. As you read these inspiring meditations, Scriptures, and prayers, be encouraged that God is for you, and he will give you everything you need to face the challenges you encounter each day.

Rest for a moment in his presence and let his grace and peace wash over you. Out of the abundance of his love and wisdom, you will find the strength to persevere in your service to others.

January

"In everything, therefore,
treat people the same way you want them to treat you,
for this is the Law and the Prophets."

Matthew 7:12 nasb

A GOOD LEADER

> "Select from all the people some capable, honest men who fear God and hate bribes. Appoint them as leaders over groups of one thousand, one hundred, fifty, and ten."
>
> EXODUS 18:21 NLT

Of all the characteristics that make a good leader, integrity is second to none. It runs alongside the ability to enjoy who we are and to protect the character that makes us unique. Also, a strong leader fears God, humbly recognizing the importance of seeking continuous help, and of growing in understanding. We must also keep ourselves unstained by the ambivalence of indecision, marginal behavior, and self-indulgence which marks the impulsive and the weak.

As you begin this year, continue to posture yourself at the feet of Christ. The Holy Spirit gives wisdom, and in waiting on him you will form the insight that is gained through practiced listening and perpetual learning. This will help you lead others and provide inspiration that only he can give. Know that you have been selected by God and be encouraged that you have started this year seeking first his kingdom. Remember the words of Christ then, that in seeking his kingdom first, other things will be added in due time.

Who has appointed you to lead, and who should lead you?

BEING PURPOSEFUL

In him we were also chosen, having been predestined according to the plan of him who works out everything in conformity with the purpose of his will, in order that we, who were the first to put our hope in Christ, might be for the praise of his glory.

EPHESIANS 1:11-12 NIV

Jesus resolved to save us and completed his task when he suffered, was killed, buried, and then resurrected. He did not relent in pursuing his goal. As a child, he sought his Father in the temple. As an adult, he purposefully suffered to the point of death. Now, as the resurrected Savior, he continues in prayer for us. When he does return as the warrior King, he will complete his goal by restoring creation to the Godhead.

When you see a person committed to his goal like Jesus was (and still is), it is worthy of admiration. As you think about this year and what you choose to purposefully do as Jesus did, be fervent in what you set your heart toward. As you do, you will naturally lead others, and may it be according to the plan of him who works to conform you to Christ for his praise and glory.

How can you encourage others to pursue Christ?

Put Together

An overseer, then, must be above reproach, the husband of
one wife, temperate, self-controlled, respectable, hospitable,
skillful in teaching, not overindulging in wine, not a bully,
but gentle, not contentious, free from the love of money.

1 TIMOTHY 3:2-3 NASB

Wow, what a person these verses describe—so collected
and put together! No one can say a bad word about them.
This leader is controlled, wise, and honored by others. They
open their wallets willingly, forgive those who do harm,
and seek to help others live in peace. They have no vices but
are filled with the Spirit of Christ.

If our friends were to be like this person, what would that
do for us? We would feel secure in our friendships with
them, for sure. We would be inspired and enjoy being with
them. Our key purpose as leaders is to not focus on being
free from the love of money or wine, but rather to employ
these attributes and to encourage those we lead to be more
like this. Our takeaway is to increasingly pursue the Holy
Spirit in our lives and to demonstrate this in our leadership
of others.

Can you perfect yourself?

LIFEGIVING TRUST

"Just as the Father raises the dead and gives them life,
so also the Son gives life to those he wants to."

JOHN 5:21 NCV

When people follow, they do so for a reason. Some seek
guidance or purpose, but many just want to have someone
tell them what to do so they can work and pay their bills.
It may be surprising, but a large number of people do not
want to lead. It is a challenge and a burden which many do
not want to bear. That alone tells you that you are called to
leadership for a reason. You have a vision, a purpose, and
the sort of gifts that are intended to be shared with those
around you.

When you think about those who follow you, what do you
provide? What can you realistically do for them outside
your natural gifts? Remember this: the Father has chosen
you, and just as he equipped his Son, he will enable you to
give beyond what you yourself are capable of. Trust him
and reside daily in the knowledge that he cares more about
those you lead than you do. Allow him to give you energy
and life to share with others because Jesus is a trustworthy
leader of leaders.

*When you look at those who follow your leadership, what do
they need from you?*

BUILDING TOGETHER

Do not neglect your gift... Be diligent in these matters;
give yourself wholly to them,
so that everyone may see your progress.

1 TIMOTHY 4:14-15 NIV

At one point in time, mankind gathered together to build a tower to heaven. So God intervened. Though we don't know the full scope of what was occurring at that time, it makes us wonder: what limits are there in humanity when we are inspired, unified, committed, hardworking, and industrious?

When we pause to think about those we lead and how we can inspire them, we must allow ourselves time to imagine what we can all accomplish together. As leaders, we need to encourage development and help others realize their potential individually as well as in a group. It is why we lead—to motivate personal growth and group productivity! Think about this: you can inspire others to come together and use their gifts to do things they could not realize on their own. It is your diligent thoughtfulness and planning that will lead others to progress.

How can you inspire unity and purpose in your teams?

ONE CRITERION

"The Father gives me the people who are mine.
Every one of them will come to me,
and I will always accept them."

JOHN 6:37 NCV

Jesus' acceptance of each one of his people is based on one criterion: faith. In our world, acceptance has become more like tolerance. We now agree to put up with beliefs and behaviors with which we don't agree. But Jesus makes it clear that he will accept anyone who comes to him. Herein lies the difference between our tolerant world and our acceptance of Christ: no one comes to Jesus without a battle. There is a cost to be received by him. When we truly allow for self-introspection, we recognize our brokenness and shame. We come to understand our true state especially as it is reflected in a holy God. His acceptance of us is unequivocal and final because to come to him means we know what we truly are like and what we honestly need.

You know your issues, and God knows them too. But you also rejoice in this, because though your sins are like scarlet, he washes you daily until you are as white as snow.

Can you take time before this busy day to rejoice in God's forgiveness and to be ready to share that forgiveness with those you lead?

RICHES OF GOODNESS

Do you despise the riches of His goodness, forbearance,
and longsuffering, not knowing that the goodness of God
leads you to repentance?

ROMANS 2:4 NKJV

The riches of God's goodness are found in the offering
of Jesus who bore our sins. Because of this sacrifice, God
is patient with us. He suffers willingly to wait for the
end of all things. He is not pleased about our continual
tendency toward sin, but in his kindness, he allows for our
repentance. None of us are without sin. We fail every day
in the standard he has set for us. When we recognize his
mercy, we can turn to him and find grace and forgiveness.
His goodness leads us to repentance.

In a similar manner, you may care for and tolerate the
failures in those you lead. This allows for growth and
maturity. Hopefully in this place of grace, people will find
the ability to rise to a new level of personal understanding
and vocational strength.

*In your walk as a leader and an influencer, how can you be
mindful of the goodness and patience which God has for you
and therefore allow that to help you make your decisions
when dealing with others?*

GOOD CHARACTER

This calls for patient endurance on the part of the people of
God who keep his commands and remain faithful to Jesus.

REVELATION 14:12 NIV

To become a person of good character is a noble quest. It
takes sacrifice, determination, and practice. It is composed
of many traits such as trustworthiness, compassion,
responsibility, and respect. Good character is formed over
time; it is not purchased or coerced into our personhood. It is
fashioned through difficulty, much like diamonds are created
through pressure and pearls grow because of an irritant. A
good character develops as we allow trouble and tribulation
to work patiently on our broken, immature selves.

We do not have to look far to find trials in life. We are
bombarded with ethical issues, relational disruptions, and
personal temptations. We are allowing good character
to form by submitting to Christ in the ways we face our
troubles. However, proper examples within our society
are lacking. We are now the most indebted, medicated,
addicted, and overweight population in known history.
This is not a society learning good character. Rather, we are
running deeper into godlessness and immaturity. Our good
characters stand as a foil to our culture because of Jesus.

*What opportunities do you have in leadership to demonstrate
a true fortitude for the good character which Christ has
established in you?*

TENSION RELIEF

One thing I ask from the LORD,
this only do I seek:
that I may dwell in the house of the LORD
all the days of my life,
to gaze on the beauty of the LORD
and to seek him in his temple.

PSALM 27:4 NIV

One of the difficulties of being in leadership is the constant pressure to rely on your resources. Whether you need to call in people or make use of something you own, your mind is probably consumed with whatever you have available at this time. But your challenges and your resources have already been brought to this moment by God. David, in his brokenness, cried out to his heavenly Father for help to abide with him. He knew the value of being in God's presence so he would have everything available to him that he would need to get through the trials he was facing in that moment.

Our comfort with today's verse is in recognizing that our brokenness is foreshadowed in the person of David. It seems that God allows us these difficulties, so we continue to fight our own natures yet always long for him. Our joys and accomplishments in this lifetime are unparalleled by the beauty and perfection that is reserved for us in eternity.

How can you fight the good fight as David did?

MORAL EXCELLENCE

"He who committed no sin,
nor was any deceit found in his mouth."

1 PETER 2:22 NASB

A virtue is a quality that has good merit and morality; a characteristic that exudes moral excellence. The virtue of truthfulness, for example, is that it demonstrates integrity, honesty, and forthrightness. Our lives can be full of trickery and deceit. Mostly we do it to ourselves, fooling our conscience into small decisions of depravity and allowing false narratives to entertain and sidetrack our minds. We ask ourselves how else we are to get by in a world that demands so much and gives so little in return. We are supposed to excel, compete well, be strong, look attractive, and be great. Yet we are typically not very great, so we make things up, bend the truth, or tell little lies.

Despite Jesus having these same struggles in his humanity while he walked on earth, because he's also God he was full of virtue. His character was unstained by any need to perform. He was content with his position in life and grounded by his relationship with his Father. This is what enabled him to be righteous and incorruptible. You can also make the Father your foundation and walk with the goal of showing others the same integrity that Jesus had as a human.

How do you lay everything at Christ's feet and allow him to guide your decisions through his Spirit?

Sports Captain

"Thomas, now that you've seen me, you believe. But there are those who have never seen me with their eyes but have believed in me with their hearts, and they will be blessed even more!"

JOHN 20:29 TPT

Being given the title of captain of a sports team is an honor. Sometimes coaches pick the least expected player for such roles, and when they do, teammates wonder about the thinking behind such a decision. What is it about that player that made them good enough to be a captain?

Empowering someone is not always about recognizing leadership ability that is already evident. Rather, it is about identifying attributes that could potentially make a great leader. After all, leaders are made, not born. A good coach can see what a team needs and equip specific people on the team who are capable of becoming that leader. Often teams have more than one captain. Some people lead well because of their attributes, and some are empowered to lead because a coach sees future abilities and wants to encourage them. Jesus has appointed you to lead.

You may recognize some of the gifts God has given you. Do you think he has more for you to find and develop in this position of leadership?

Choose Today

"If you refuse to serve the LORD, then choose today whom you will serve. But as for me and my family, we will serve the LORD."

JOSHUA 24:15 NLT

There is something inspirational about a decisive person; they proactively and confidently make decisions and take responsibility for their domain. The impetuous are foolish and make rash decisions while reacting, but those who are decisive with wisdom are admired. This is not a matter of semantics, but rather about the ability to weigh a situation and employ experience and wisdom. The impulsive person does not think before they act. The decisive one considers their way and takes action. This is what makes a leader stand out.

However, our decisiveness can be paralyzed by fear of failure. We can allow our minds to start comparing and worrying about the consequences. We can start to dread the ridicule with results with a wrong decision, especially as leaders. These fears and doubts are relieved when we surrender our decisions to Christ and recognize that our hope lays in him and his final word over us. Ultimately, when we serve the Lord, our choices are committed to him. We serve him and him first, and by submitting our hearts to him we can trust the Holy Spirit to help us in our decisiveness.

Can you trust his Spirit to lead you in your current position?

HOPE SUPPLY

"I am the resurrection and the life. The one who believes in me will live, even though they die; and whoever lives by believing in me will never die."

JOHN 11:25-26 NIV

There is something incredible about hope and placing our beliefs in something that gives us strength in the moment. We see people around us demoralized, confused, and uncertain, and yet we have the answers so many people are looking for. We have the certainty that we will be resurrected one day and that our lives are in the hands of a completely faithful leader. His promises are certain, and his Word has never failed.

Your leadership position can also give others hope and that can feel overwhelming at times. It is a weight that not all people can bear. But you can because you rely on the greatest leader. Jesus is the one who will strengthen you and as you lean into him you can remind yourself of the promises of his Word. The courage you receive from his truth enables you to equip others with that beautiful hope.

How does your understanding of his promises help you share his hope with others?

WELL PLEASED

When Jesus was baptized, immediately he went up from the water, and behold, the heavens were opened to him, and he saw the Spirit of God descending like a dove and coming to rest on him; and behold, a voice from heaven said, "This is my beloved Son, with whom I am well pleased."

MATTHEW 3:16-17 ESV

When you consider the life of Jesus, you start to realize that he did not spend energy working to please anyone. He even suffered bad opinions about himself willingly and with admirable strength. We typically don't suffer well unless it gains us something; one of those "somethings" is the approval of others. We work long hours and boast about our achievements as we seek the adulation of others.

Oh, how hard we work to gain approval! Everyone does it. We may attempt to be approved by some in authority, peers, family members, friends, or social groups. There is a lot of approval to be earned out there, so we must work hard to get it. Our desire for approval is not all bad; it is in us to drive us toward Christ. Ultimately, and what will satisfy us completely and properly, is to know his approval of us. And he does approve of us as we seek to do his will. He loves the fact that you are seeking him now and enjoys the time you spend in his presence.

What makes you valuable to God?

A Satisfied Life

*I know what it is to be in need, and I know what it is to
have plenty. I have learned the secret of being content
in any and every situation, whether well fed or hungry,
whether living in plenty or in want.*

PHILIPPIANS 4:12 NIV

Leadership carries the weight of needing to ensure that
those you serve are content. It is troubling at times to
have followers who are upset, especially if it happens
frequently. We all know this ends in attrition. But teaching
contentment is not all on us as leaders because we can only
influence those we lead. We do not ultimately own the
responsibility for the attitudes of others.

Our best efforts for the positive influence of others comes
in how we exemplify a satisfied life in Christ. Contentment
forms when we recognize that God is our everything
and our spirit is awakened to that need. We know who
the provider of all that we truly need is! We look to him
alone as our source. But understanding that premise
and knowing it at a heart level are two different things!
Discipline yourself to depend on God. If you struggle
with dependence on God, try fasting as that can provoke
our spirits toward God and learned contentment. Be
encouraged to take time to learn the secret of a hidden life
in Christ, the abstained satisfied soul.

Does your team look at you and see that you are content?

PRIVATE GENEROSITY

Whoever is generous to the poor lends to the LORD,
and he will repay him for his deed.

PROVERBS 19:17 ESV

When you are in leadership, you have to make decisions that, at times, no one else takes part in and no one else may notice. These are not bad decisions; they are just what need to be done. You may make good decisions that no one gives you credit for or even notices.

Take comfort in the fact that God notices both your thoughts and your actions. He sees those moments when you give beyond your own capabilities or make choices that can impact the bottom line for the betterment of others. God's greatest concern is not money but in how you use money to affect the lives of others. He loves integrity in his people and observing the decisions you make as you seek him first in all things. Continue to allow his Spirit to lead you and listen for those quiet directions which he wants to give you. Know that in time, he will reward you greatly for your private and purposeful obedience.

To whom specifically does God want you to be generous?

STRENGTH TO CHANGE

He gives more grace. Therefore it says,
"God opposes the proud but gives grace to the humble."

JAMES 4:6 ESV

A hard heart can form quickly through repeated emotional trauma. This trauma can come from many sources, but it's often most painfully experienced at the hands of the members of our families. We learn so much early on in our lives and it can be hard to soften our hearts so that we can hear God as we get older if we remain in a place of pain.

God is gracious, and his patience allows us to change slowly over time if we learn humility and grace. He will lift up those who are bowed down. He is kind. He loves unconditionally because he is love. His grace empowers us in our weaknesses, for that is what grace does: it allows weakness to exist so we can be strengthened by it. Grace gives us the strength we need to change. Let us become leaders who demonstrate, from the inside out, the goodness of God's graciousness.

When you are upset how do you remain gracious to others?

SWEET RESPITE

You are free from the power of sin and have become slaves
of God. Now you do those things that lead to holiness and
result in eternal life.

ROMANS 6:22 NLT

Have you pondered what life would be like without sin? Sin
is not just a state of being it is also a causal effect. We live
in a sinful world and sin dwells within man which results
in sinful man making sinful choices. It is not escapable in
this lifetime. Jesus came and defeated sin and its power
over us. Its power was death which is produced in us from
inception. As followers of Jesus, we are no longer slaves to
sin and therefore we can and do choose righteousness. It is
a beautiful thing!

However, every day we still battle against sin. Imagine no
longer fighting the propensity to sin. What a great relief
that will be! It is unfathomable. We have an eternity with
God and without sin. Every choice we will make will be
the right one, not in defiance to God but in alignment with
him. What sweet respite that will be. Add to this the beauty
of being a new creation with healed and whole bodies,
enjoying our relationships forevermore. We can truly get
excited at our prospects for eternal life!

*What excites you most about being freed from the power
of sin?*

SOURCE OF ALL

O God in Zion, to you even silence is praise!
You who answers prayer,
all of humanity comes before you with their requests.

PSALM 65:1-2 TPT

You can imagine the trouble your life would become if all the world approached you with their problems. It is trouble enough leading a small organization or even a family! When we become overwhelmed with issues in leadership, we can quickly dismiss what we deem as smaller matters, but then we are also dismissing the people who bring those matters to light. It is important for us to be approachable to all people if we want to keep a pulse on what is happening in our organizations. The larger the group we lead, the greater the help we need.

Even so, notice in this verse that God needs no help. He can handle all the requests and all the problems. He is the source of life for all of mankind. He is also your source. You can go to him with confidence. As a chosen leader, you are an instrument to others as a source of God's strength.

How can you trust that God will equip you to remain approachable? Can you rely on him to give you the necessary wisdom to deal with whatever comes your way?

THE CORE FEATURE

Faith is the assurance of things hoped for,
the conviction of things not seen.

HEBREWS 11:1 ESV

When God establishes a leader, he looks for people who will follow him with dynamic and passionate fervor. Some are fearful at first, and they lack faith and boldness. It seems that all make mistakes, but each one ends up being brave servants of God.

Mankind may look at the people God chose in the Bible and comment that they were extreme in some way or another. They spoke of or accomplished things that are sometimes impossible to believe. But that is the nature of leadership. It requires men and women who are bold in the face of adversity, and courageous enough to pursue their dreams. People who lead like this are driven by a core feature—hope. They overcome mistakes because they have the drive to accomplish what they set out to do. As a leader, you have this hope and conviction. You aspire to inspire, and you have within you the belief to accomplish what you hope for.

Can you allow God to take what you have, and use it to pass hope on to those you lead?

Perfect Blend

We who are strong must be considerate of those who are sensitive about things like this. We must not just please ourselves. We should help others do what is right and build them up in the Lord. For even Christ didn't live to please himself.

Romans 15:1-3 NLT

People who are seen as successful in leadership may be the very people who stand out in crowds, who are charismatic, strong, forceful, loud, or even self-promoting. Yet, a thoughtful leader is one who is considerate of others, kind in words and actions, and selfless. There is a plethora of these traits reflected in Christ although he was never self-promoting. Jesus only promoted the Father.

When it suited God's purposes, Jesus was a crowd-pleaser. He performed miracles, lambasted the Pharisees for their hypocrisy, and defended the poor, sick, and elderly. But there was a caring, unselfish, quiet side to him. He comforted his disciples, taught children, and cared for the ill. He was truly the perfect man and the righteous Son of God.

Though you may not be like Jesus yet, can you aim to do the things he did in the way he did them, using the Spirit as your guide?

CONNECTION MATTERS

Physical training is of some value, but godliness has value for all things, holding promise for both the present life and the life to come.

1 TIMOTHY 4:8 NIV

We should be healthy, exercising our bodies and eating well. All of us want to remain vigorous as long as we live on the earth. Our bodies are also the temple of the Holy Spirit so we should treat them with respect and appreciation. When it comes to exercise and healthy eating, we want to do right by ourselves, but we will also fight genetics and the fallen state of earthly life.

Therefore, balance is necessary and less comparison amongst us is critical. Our efforts for good health are to be focused on godliness first and understanding that which will last into eternity. It does not mean we disregard ourselves, but we need to keep our focus on what matters most: our connection and obedience to God. It is important to note that God cares about the whole person, and we should as well when we lead others. Sometimes we are so focused on accomplishments that we forget to understand that we all need that connection in our relationships to God, ourselves, and others.

If you make time for those you lead in godliness ahead of or in conjunction with your own physical training, how can you encourage them to connect to the same priority?

SHIFT WORK

Lord, hear my prayer,
listen to my cry for mercy;
in your faithfulness and righteousness
come to my relief.

PSALM 143:1 NIV

Many things exasperate us as leaders, and maybe nothing frustrates us more than attending to disrupted relationships. Especially troubling is when broken friendships, work relationships, or even marriages cause delays in our accomplishments and productivity. We may also face situations when exhausted people are a danger to themselves and others. Perhaps we are lacking the resources to hire more staff or enlist more help. Ugh; more delays are inevitable. These things grate at us and weary us. In the workplace, shift work was developed to help tired workers because long hours were recognized as unsafe and unprofitable. The reprieve of shifts allows workers to come back refreshed and more effective.

Do leaders have the ability to take shifts off? Yes, in much the same way the Lord provides a place of relief for his leaders to be refreshed and renewed. It requires discipline to leave our responsibilities behind us for a period of rest. God, however, has specific grace for you to do that. He not only promises to bring you respite, but he is faithful and right in his responses to your burdens.

How can you find relief as you cry out to God?

DIGGING FOR GOLD

All the ways of a person are clean in his own sight,
But the LORD examines the motives.

PROVERBS 16:2 NASB

Determining what motivates us can be like digging for gold. If you have ever watched gold miners at work, it takes some hard labor and experience. It's usually a sacrifice, but it ends up with great rewards. If you know what motivates you, going after it will give you passion and joy—and potentially a good reason to live.

One of the top motivators for leaders is to have a sense of accomplishment—to build something great. If a goal is set and completed, there is a release of endorphins which brings pleasure. When accomplishments add up to a large success it brings great satisfaction. God put this desire in us, and he very much wants us to be motivated first to seek him. As we read his Word and dwell in the presence of his Spirit, we find our enthusiasm aligning with his. Our joy is completed in his joy, and we find a satisfaction that is pure contentment. When we chase after him, God aligns our purpose with roles and tasks that we fulfill and then we find a great reason to live!

What gets you up and going in the morning?

KEENLY AWARE

What is mankind that you are mindful of them,
human beings that you care for them?

PSALM 8:4 NIV

Have you ever watched someone holding a coffee or
some other beverage and they start to get so engrossed in
their conversation that they forget that they are holding
something that can spill? Suddenly there is a stark reminder
as they drop or misplace their drink, and usually people or
equipment are affected. But if you remind them before they
drop anything, they are very thankful.

Imagine if you could be on top of every possible accident
wherever you are. People would be amazed. That is what
God is like. He is aware of absolutely everything. This
amazes us if we allow ourselves to dwell on this great
feature of his. God is so mindful of us that he is conscious
of our every moment and every movement. Imagine
keeping track of that many incidences on planet earth. Even
so, he doesn't control us like robots. He engages with us at
our invitation. He has the awareness and the power; he just
wants our invitation first. Invite him into your day and let
him lead you as you lead others.

*How does God get your attention? Journal those moments so
you can think about them later.*

THE COURAGE HORMONE

Do not neglect to do good and to share what you have,
for such sacrifices are pleasing to God.

HEBREWS 13:16 ESV

Leaders take risks. They dive in when no one else will, and they inspire from the frontlines. There is a natural release of dopamine, serotonin, endorphins, and oxytocin—the four feel-good hormones—when you do this. When we hear a baby cry or someone scream, if there is a siren going off, or if we hear the yelp of an animal, we are alerted to trouble and our adrenaline—the courage hormone—kicks in. It grasps our attention. If it is clear we are the only help available, we jump into action.

People who save others say they are not heroes and that they just did what anyone else would do. This statement is not far from the truth. We were all made to be helpful and caring. The only difference may be in one's ability to overcome fear, and that is what leaders do. In our day-to-day lives, however, we need people to show up, be courteous, cooperate, and care. You can create that culture today.

Can you look for those people who may need help? Can you engage those you lead with encouraging words specific to them?

UNIVERSAL COLLABORATION

Just as each of us has one body with many members, and these members do not all have the same function, so in Christ we, though many, form one body, and each member belongs to all the others.

ROMANS 12:4-5 NIV

In a world of independence, ethnic turmoil, and global market crashes, we have also witnessed universal collaboration. During the recent pandemic, we saw the world stop and focus on one global issue. Humans cooperated on a level we have not seen before: globally, we isolated, masked, and exhibited behavior which demonstrated general concern for one another. There were lots of questions and varying opinions, but the reality is that the pandemic saw many problems set aside and entire populations focus on the most urgent issue. Out of that shift, a sense of global community and care has arisen. Perhaps healing can begin?

Cooperation is emphasized in our faith as something God desires for all of us. It can occur amongst the people you lead. They will need clear direction and purpose in order to see how they contribute to a greater mission. In Christ, you have been equipped to lead and to give vision to others.

What helps you look to God for his wisdom and to trust in his leadership?

EQUAL MATURITY

Speaking the truth in love, we will grow to become in every respect the mature body of him who is the head, that is, Christ. From him the whole body, joined and held together by every supporting ligament, grows and builds itself up in love, as each part does its work.

EPHESIANS 4:15-16 NIV

There is a leadership lesson in this great picture that Paul gives here in today's verse. It is helpful in explaining that it is the whole body of Christ that matures and not just its parts. In some ways, each part needs to mature equally for each to contribute fully. A ligament must be mature enough to handle a strong muscle otherwise it will snap. Similarly, bones need to be strong enough to support the weight of the flesh. There is a lot of work to make a group of people unified!

Focusing on one person at the expense of others can contribute to dysfunction, but developing each person in their gifts will cohesively strengthen the whole body. As you consider those under your leadership, attempt to be aware of what each person needs in order to continue their development and to bravely broach the difficulties on the path of progress.

What helps you encourage growth in others even when a hard conversation is needed?

Full Promise

Patient endurance is what you need now,
so that you will continue to do God's will.
Then you will receive all that he has promised.

HEBREWS 10:36 NLT

The great pleasure of leading is witnessing people being raised up to take your place and essentially becoming redundant. We develop people so they can competently do what an organization needs. If they do it well, we promote them. The reward for them is to one day take our place. We know we are not eternal in our roles, and if we hold on to our positions like we are, we will inhibit healthy growth.

The best thing we can do as leaders is find people we trust who can handle the job, and then give it all over to them in time. This is what God wants to do in us too. Jesus ascended so that the Spirit could dwell in God's new leadership—us. It is a kingdom principle. Just as God is incredibly patient and waits for us to mature, so we also need to be patient and wait for the full promise of all that God has while he continues to help us develop into who we need to be.

How long can you see yourself in your current role? Do you have someone in mind to take your place?

Spoken Word

Everything you speak to me is like joyous treasure,
filling my life with gladness.

Psalm 119:111 TPT

We live in a video-first world. The saying, "A picture is
worth a thousand words," is true. As our eyes scan a canvas
and take in colors and shapes, a story is told. Pictures come
to life for us in the telling of that story. We now regularly
watch moving pictures, or movies, which come complete
with creative effects and variances of sound.

But we must not discount what God designed into our
beautiful minds: people evoke emotion through spoken or
visual stories and elicit images which create thousands of
individual ideas that are tailored by each person doing the
listening or the watching. The joyous treasure of the spoken
word that fills us with gladness is not found in something men
created, but rather it is found in the Creator and in the minds
that he gave us. God created it all, and as we learn to delight in
him, we will find fulfillment in him. The overflow of a fulfilled
life is poured out on those with whom it is shared.

Can you see how God uses your excess to bless those you lead?

INSPIRED TO IMITATE

Be imitators of me,
as I am of Christ.

1 CORINTHIANS 11:1 ESV

Leadership 101: if you cannot mentor people who want to imitate you then you should not be leading. Perhaps people do not want to imitate you in all areas of life, but certainly they should in the areas of leadership and expertise that you hold. This is a call to ensure that we understand our influence over others, that we are a good example, that we have integrity, that we demonstrate humility because we know we will fail at times, that we know how to listen well, and that we serve sincerely.

We have a responsibility to demonstrate this for the organization we lead because we are disciples of Christ. And what we know of Christ is this: his success was established on his dependency upon his Father. As he relied upon God to strengthen him, so we must rely on Christ to help us. We are fully equipped to lead and to have people imitate us just as we aspire to imitate Christ.

What is it about you that people want to imitate, and what inspires them to follow you?

FEBRUARY

Be diligent to present yourself approved to God
as a worker who does not need to be ashamed,
accurately handling the word of truth.

2 TIMOTHY 2:15 NASB

RECOGNIZED VALUE

Recognize the value of every person and continually show love to every believer. Live your lives with great reverence and in holy awe of God. Honor your rulers.

1 PETER 2:17 TPT

What is your worth, or where do you find your value? Some psychologists say that the concept of self-esteem leads a person to negatively value themselves. It means you rate yourself based on a scale that seems to move depending upon how you accomplish tasks or how you relate to others. When things are going well, subjectively speaking, you have higher esteem. Yet it only takes a few knocks and bumps, and your esteem can take you down dark, sundry trails. What is your worth when relationships are not doing well or you are not feeling accomplished?

We are each esteemed by God. All humans are treasured. He loves his creation, and we are valued by him. We should never arrive at the place of utter despair because we are the recipients of God's great love. Life can knock us down, but good leadership can encourage us to see our worth with God's eyes.

How can you show others that they are valued?

PAUSE AND CONSIDER

The LORD merely spoke,
and the heavens were created.
He breathed the word,
and all the stars were born.

PSALM 33:6 NLT

When life is stressful and our decisions are weighing on us, it is good to pause and consider what God has created and how he made it all. Nature has a way of easing our burdens when we get outside and engage with it. God designed the world around us that way. It also helps to recognize his authority over all things, and to remind ourselves that he spoke the Word and life was created. Our efforts to create come with taxing thoughts, great labor, and varying results. God worked with ease, and what he made was good because he is good. He is also able to make our lives good when we follow him.

It is important, even necessary, for mankind to pause and take time to consider what God has made. When we do, we begin to realize how incredible he is. It brings forth in us expressions of praise and worship because he is worthy.

Consider what you have, what God has made through you, and what you can praise him for.

JUBILANT

Let the fields be jubilant, and everything in them;
let all the trees of the forest sing for joy.
Let all creation rejoice before the LORD, for he comes,
he comes to judge the earth.
He will judge the world in righteousness
and the peoples in his faithfulness.

PSALM 96:12-13 NIV

We can easily get into our routines and form habits in order
to create normalcy in our lives. It helps us if we have a
certain way to accomplish repetitive tasks to better handle
life. But even if we settle into these comfortable routines
and we do well checking off the boxes, it's also good to learn
to adjust to uncomfortable circumstances. It's spiritually
healthy to learn to embrace foreign customs, languages,
and foods which we never would have encountered without
some effort on our part.

Scripture talks about how easily we are beset by sin and
entangled by it. We may not even realize that sin has
entrapped us. Most of us know very little about captivity
and mistreatment, so the feeling of delight at being set free
is hard to grasp. When we consider what it means to be
so full of joy that our bodies express it without hesitation,
what would have happened to cause us to be so jubilant?
Those whom the Son sets free are free indeed!

*Since God has set you free, what can you do express your
jubilation?*

DILIGENT WORKERS

Since you are waiting for these, be diligent to be found by
him without spot or blemish, and at peace.

2 PETER 3:14 ESV

It was a hot day to be working outside with temperatures
rising to 100° Fahrenheit. He lifted heavy bags one by
one as sweat dripped from his head and his body became
soaked with his efforts. As the day dragged on, the weight
of the bags intensified, and the draining heat started to take
its toll. His body was exhausted, but still he kept slugging
away. He worked sixteen hours, lifted several thousand
pounds, and walked seventeen miles. He consumed four
liters of water. He was dirty and drenched with sweat, yet he
walked proudly as he left for home.

Diligent workers are difficult to come by. Their focus is not
on self-gratification but on maintaining endurance and
having the fortitude to complete the task. The reward for
people with this trait is found in consistent employment,
recognition for their efforts, and, like yourself, promotion
into leadership roles. Be encouraged that your patient
endurance and tenacious diligence will pay off and place
you in a position to acknowledge others similarly.

Who is the hard worker you can appreciate today?

BEING FORTHRIGHT

Having put away falsehood, let each one of you speak the truth with his neighbor, for we are members one of another.

EPHESIANS 4:25 ESV

A key element to building a strong organization and membership base is to cultivate a sense of camaraderie amongst those members. Having a group of people who are aligned in what they want to accomplish and how to traverse the path to get there is distinctly productive. And when people truly believe in each other and support one another through victory and adversity, it is a pleasure to watch. This doesn't happen unless the members are real with each other.

When vulnerability leads to authenticity in an organization, closeness and synergy can occur. But this does not come from the new members or the inexperienced. It takes leaders with the inner strength of Christ, as well as the patience and faith that allows for others to fail, recover, and grow. This is your opportunity to demonstrate how to be forthright but to do so with love and compassion.

Take time today to search for an example of Jesus speaking in a straightforward manner, yet with love. Aspire to emulate him in your leadership mannerisms.

ESTABLISHED EXAMPLE

"The Father loves the Son and shows him everything he
is doing. In fact, the Father will show him how to do even
greater works than healing this man. Then you will be
truly astonished."

JOHN 5:20 NLT

Leadership is not just about being gifted with that quality.
We actually learn to be leaders by emulating others who
are successful as leaders themselves. Jesus was educated by
watching what his Father said and did. He saw his actions,
heard his words, and knew his heart. Because of his close
connection to the Father, Jesus was able to demonstrate a
likeness that no other can accomplish. He truly is one with
his Father.

As we go about leading others, they too will be looking to
us as established examples of what the healthy management
of people and resources look like. We have been given a
great gift that can do harm or benefit others. A lot depends
on us as leaders, and as much as our best efforts will
sometimes fail, when we emulate Christ by seeking the
Father's heart, we will do good.

*What are the successful traits of the leadership of Jesus which
you now emulate or can learn to emulate?*

PUSHED TO GROW

You created my inmost being;
you knit me together in my mother's womb.

PSALM 139:13 NIV

Did you envision yourself in the position you are in now when you were a child? Teachers like to ask children to try to project or dream about what they want to do when they grow up. Parents ask their children as they near the end of their high school years about their career aspirations and hope those goals won't waste finances on schooling that ends in a futile career.

Now we lead others and hopefully accomplish the very thing we were made for. It is not an easy role being a leader. You have to speak up, you have to push others, and you have to take risks that no one else is willing to take. But as a leader, you do it and you encourage others to be brave in doing so as well. In fact, you may even help others step out beyond their safe places and become the people that God wanted them to be. Don't dismiss your imperfect impact in Gods perfect plan!

Who do you see in your organization that can be pushed to grow beyond where they are now? What can you do to encourage them?

DELIBERATE STEPS

*Give careful thought to the paths for your feet
and be steadfast in all your ways.*

PROVERBS 4:26 NIV

Being deliberate means to carefully consider our actions before taking the necessary steps toward a goal. Being deliberate is a strength in those who are patient. When we develop a habit of making decisions this way, it can often lead to success in life's pursuits. It is likely the reason we are where we are right now, leading others as a calling from God. People who generally fail, not just in one momentary act but in a lifetime of repeated failures, tend to be those who act irrationally and hastily. It seems that an element of chance runs parallel to success.

Risks are important to leaders, but the decision to take or not take a risk does not require impulsivity. In fact, good risks are meticulously considered only after seeking the wisdom of God and seasoned advisors. Sure, we may not know ahead of time the outcomes when we are making certain decisions, but there is a good chance that with resolute determination and steadfastness, we will bring about the outcome we are looking for especially as our lives are submitted to Christ.

What processes have you embraced for making deliberate, steadfast decisions? What steps do you take to submit those decisions to Christ?

SHARED GOAL

All the people were amazed and said,
"Perhaps this man is the Son of David!"

MATTHEW 12:23 NCV

One of the most difficult achievements of a leader is to bring a group of people together and have them agree to a shared vision and embark on the process to accomplish it. It is very satisfying, however, to see inspiration turn into productivity and result in a completed goal. This is invigorating both for us as leaders and for the whole team who worked to accomplish the goal. Leaders are encouraged when backed by people who believe in them and in their vision. Team members are encouraged (even spiritually) as they meet a shared goal with solid leadership.

Imagine what Jesus felt like as he performed miracles and spoke the truth with God's authority, yet experienced conflict and dissension as people still doubted. Sure, lots of people expressed amazement and wonder, but there were still plenty that doubted him. Today, as in that day, Jesus has his doubters. We as leaders know what that is like. People hear what we are saying, and despite proof of our integrity and capabilities, they still don't believe. Trust in the process that God has you on and continue to lean into him as Christ did. He will finish the good work he began in each of us.

What do you find amazing about Christ's accomplishments in the gospels and today?

Not an Outsider

"I will also bless the foreigners
who commit themselves to the Lord,
who serve him and love his name…
I will bring them to my holy mountain of Jerusalem
and will fill them with joy in my house of prayer…
my temple will be called a house of prayer for all nations."

Isaiah 56:6-7 nlt

God always includes the outsider. He sees those who are weak, needy, and helpless. He cares deeply about them. That is his heart. Anyone, no matter what their standing is, can come to him and he will accept them compassionately and lovingly as his own.

The key to obtaining God's love and leadership is that we need to come to him, and we need to desire his help; it is a requirement that we recognize our state of humility, our sin nature, and our need of God's grace. In response, he promises unfailing love and strength. These promises are for you, too, as his follower and his chosen worker. As you come to him in humility, he will lift you up and give you peace and endurance.

How has Christ's consistent love for you enabled you to love other people?

TACTFUL SPEECH

Let your conversation be always full of grace, seasoned with
salt, so that you may know how to answer everyone.

COLOSSIANS 4:6 NIV

Jesus was consistently maligned, yet he did not defend
himself. Rather, he pointed to the Father as the authority
for his own words and work. How was he able to be so
patient and tolerant of the ignorant? Being able to hold
your tongue is a great feat. James writes that the tongue is
untamable: it is a match to start a fire and a rudder to steer
the boat. But when we are filled with grace, we can learn to
slow down our responses and be more sensitive.

Tactfulness is about exhibiting diplomacy and showing
sensitivity in a situation that could easily become enflamed.
Grace is critical because it allows for others to make
mistakes and for us as mature leaders to extend favor
and tact. At times we have had to be brash and to speak
up boldly. There may have been times when we have not
seasoned our words with grace. We seek God's forgiveness
for those moments. We trust him to cover our broken
leadership with his perfection.

How do you employ tactful measures in your speech?

A Fruitful End

Love is as strong as death,
its jealousy as enduring as the grave.
Love flashes like fire,
the brightest kind of flame.
Many waters cannot quench love,
nor can rivers drown it.

Song of Solomon 8:6-7 nlt

Passion is required to move us to action. None of us have pursued something we really wanted without a motivating desire to fuel us. It's a part of the human condition and God put it in us all. The beauty of this is that we can, because of this shared experience, identify hunger within those we lead. We can assist in furthering others in what they do under our leadership and for God. It is how we can help drive results and get more accomplished. However, we want to be careful because that which starts with a common thirst can quickly become quenched. Some cravings are satiated rapidly but to what purpose?

Desire starts us on the road, but patient endurance is what gets us to the true destination. God's love goes beyond simple yearnings and demonstrates the faithfulness of the rising sun. He shows us that we need both to get moving: passion and durability must co-exist to last throughout the whole journey and right to its fruitful end.

What are you most passionate about right now?

SEEKING REASONS

"Fear not, for I have redeemed you;
I have called you by name, you are mine."

ISAIAH 43:1 ESV

Our existence on this planet is tied to the union of the two people whom we call our parents. Some of us don't know who our parents are and others of us know only one of them. Some of us know both of our parents and they are still present in our lives. Our families give us a sense of identity and belonging which help ground us throughout our lives, but it is never enough. We need more than just our families; we need a purpose too. Work can bring us that in some sense, but ultimately each of us needs to know we belong, and that God has preordained us with a unique purpose. He is literally our everything. He is our Redeemer.

You, as a leader, have been gifted with a significant role to play in the lives of others. Your leadership strengths are important to guide others in the pursuit of their own unique purposes. Your position in their lives can help stimulate a deeper search for God. As you acknowledge this privilege, lean upon God to help you lead.

How can you encourage others in their pursuit of God?

WHO LOVE IS

Such love has no fear, because perfect love expels all fear.
If we are afraid, it is for fear of punishment, and this shows
that we have not fully experienced his perfect love. We love
each other because he loved us first.

1 JOHN 4:18-19 NLT

It is hard to imagine a world without love, and on this
special day we celebrate it globally. Though it does not have
clear origins, one story is that Valentine was a martyred
priest in the third century who secretly married lovers
before the men were pressed into military service. The
emperor at the time believed single men made better
warriors and denied marriage to all young men. Saint
Valentine gave up his life for love.

We don't think of Jesus' love as romantic because it is far
more encompassing than simply idealistic passion. Jesus
is like Saint Valentine, however, because he also lost his
life for love. Jesus' love is patient, kind, not envious, not
boastful, humble, selfless, temperate, forgiving, virtuous,
truthful, protecting, trusting, hopeful, and persevering. It is
a raw and powerful love that comes from deep within God.
It is who he is.

*How can you replicate these characteristics of love in your
own leadership?*

RELIABLE FORTRESS

Teach those who are rich in this world not to be proud and not to trust in their money, which is so unreliable. Their trust should be in God, who richly gives us all we need for our enjoyment.

1 TIMOTHY 6:17 NLT

When we are successful, we often rely upon ourselves to see something through to completion. It is natural to trust in yourself to accomplish your goals when you have strong self-reliance and the belief that you have the necessary skills and traits. But it is also a subtle trap that can end in pride; and pride is an abomination to God. It takes a holy strength to rely upon God ahead of ourselves. And though we understand that wealth is unreliable, by the time we reach the stage of our lives when we hold positions of authority, hopefully we have also come to realize that we are fallible and prone to failure.

The opportunity we have to demonstrate to others a beautiful humility and dependence on God is necessary to be a person who succeeds for God's purposes. Christ is our reliable fortress. He never lets us down nor is he weak. He is everything we need to live a life of purpose as well as satisfaction and joy.

Because God satisfies you fully, how can you shift your vision away from earthly things to him?

PATH OF SOBRIETY

The end of all things is near.
Therefore, be alert and of sober mind so that you may pray.

1 PETER 4:7 NIV

When completing a project, especially as time draws near to the end, there is a focus and clarity that takes over other distractions. Being devoted to one goal becomes easier as the pressure of closure becomes imminent. Similarly, God calls us to be aware of our current environment and the spiritual atmosphere that surrounds us. Are we aware of the world and its shaking foundation? His return is drawing near, and we need sobriety to think clearly and act quickly when it becomes necessary.

Jesus makes it clear that we will not know the day or the hour, but he tells his disciples that the seasons will be evident for anyone who is paying attention. With all that is occurring on the earth and within mankind, we must be awake as a people. We need men and women in leadership to help believers on this path of sobriety. You have been raised up for such a time as this. Embrace what Jesus has given to you as his chosen gift for you, and lead others wisely.

What in your life promotes sobriety in preparation for Jesus' return?

JUST BECAUSE

We must not become tired of doing good.
We will receive our harvest of eternal life at the right time
if we do not give up.

GALATIANS 6:9 NCV

Receiving a reward is often related to accomplishing a
task, completing a project, or winning an event. In other
words, something has been done. How often do we receive
rewards for not doing anything? There may be a few times.
A good father might call a child over once in a while and
give them something they love, simply saying, "This is just
for being you." No achievement was accomplished, no task
was completed, and no competition was won. It is just for
being you.

Jesus made it clear that we do not have to do any works
to receive our reward of eternal life. Those who believe
are rewarded for their righteousness. It is through faith
in Christ as our substitutional sacrifice that we will be
rewarded. Wow! What grace and favor we receive when
we clearly do not deserve it! No task was accomplished, no
project was completed, no event was won. Just faith was
necessary.

*Today as you think about what you deserve before a holy
God, remind yourself about what Christ paid. Are you filled
with joy and gratitude for his sacrifice?*

Serve in Compassion

The LORD God said, "It is not good for the man to be alone.
I will make a helper who is just right for him."

GENESIS 2:18 NLT

No matter what menial role we take on, even if it is just to
serve water, helpfulness is demonstrated in cooperating in
order to complete a project or a purpose. When you look
at the team of people you lead and serve, how do you see
them? It's possible that you don't see each person equally as
it is natural to connect with some people easier than others.
That can compel us to value some more than others. Yet
God sees each of us and values us all without any partiality.
He judges us based on his high standards and none of us
are counted as righteous; we all fall short. However, because
of Christ we are all justified and sanctified. He is our
greatest helper, and his position is exemplified through his
great sacrifice. He even washed the feet of those for whom
he died!

When we seek to serve one another in compassion and
love, we are cooperating with God's purpose. This is what
God calls us to do as a body of believers, whether it is in the
workplace or in our homes, on the field or at our church.
No matter what the role is that we take on, he calls us to be
helpful.

Who can you serve this week?

GAME OF PERSPECTIVES

They won't be afraid of bad news;
their hearts are steady because they trust the LORD.

PSALM 112:7 NCV

What do we do when someone asks if we want the good news or the bad news first? Usually, we steel ourselves and consider what these bits of news could be. If we can prepare ourselves for the worst, perhaps it will not be as devastating when we actually hear. Most of this is obviously contextual. Everything can be a whole lot lighter if the question is delivered as a joke. It's all a game of perspectives.

When it comes to the end of the world or the final days of our lives, however, it can be hard to have a positive view. One big difference is felt in knowing God and having faith that his promises are true. We do not have to be anxious about it at all if we know the character and person of Jesus Christ. We can have certainty in how everything ends.

What stirs your heart to remain steadfast in a world of turmoil?

In the Face of Fear

In the fear of the LORD there is strong confidence,
And his children will have refuge.

PROVERBS 14:26 NASB

What is the most difficult decision you have made so far
in your leadership? What helped you overcome the fear of
failure or the sense of shame you may have experienced if
you made the wrong choice? For those who trust in God,
there is a confidence that, despite making a tough decision,
we will be all right. Sure, the experience many humble us,
or we may wonder at the end result, but being unafraid
of making those difficult decisions is all about having
confidence and boldness, pushing aside fear, and trusting
in God.

People look to us to know what to do. They expect us to act
confidently. Knowing this can be a weight on us, but when
we lay that burden on him, we can trust that he will help
guide us. Have strong confidence that God is with you and
be bold. He helps those who look to him.

*Who or what do you trust so you are unafraid and can work
through the difficult decisions in leadership?*

PERFECT PEACE

"You keep him in perfect peace
whose mind is stayed on you,
because he trusts in you."

ISAIAH 26:3 ESV

Being confident in your words is a valuable attribute that
can really make a difference in your confidence level. When
you tell people you'll be there or you'll take care of it, and
people know you will, they trust you. Being trustworthy
is something that we want to aspire to as leaders. We want
to demonstrate a commitment and consistency in our
statements that allows people around us to feel confident in
who we are, what we say, and what we do.

God is trustworthy. He is not a liar. He is faithful. He is
not only able to do what he says, but he is dependable,
honorable, and consistent. He is the perfect leader. If we
learn to rely on his trustworthiness, we can be at peace
because we know who he is and that his Word is true.

*In your life, how do you see God demonstrating his
trustworthiness?*

IN THE STORM

Fully awake, he rebuked the storm and shouted to the sea, "Hush! Be still!" All at once the wind stopped howling and the water became perfectly calm.

MARK 4:39 TPT

Just before this verse Jesus was asleep like there was nothing to worry about. Anyone who has been in a storm on the ocean or has even seen one, knows that it is a wonder Jesus was able to sleep. We know that God tests us, and this incident certainly seems to have been a test for the disciples. They even questioned if Jesus cared enough to spare their lives. They did know, however, who to appeal to when they were on the verge of catastrophe.

When you are in a state of chaos in your life and all that surrounds you is worry and fear of the unknown, turn to Jesus. He is right there in the middle of the storm, waiting to bring calm to your chaos. He is trustworthy and true to his Word. Sure, you may face difficulties, and he doesn't promise an easy life. He promises joy and peace because of or in spite of your circumstances! That only comes by trusting in him.

How do you invite Jesus into your storm?

ETERNAL RETIREMENT

The LORD is good and his love endures forever;
his faithfulness continues through all generations.

PSALM 100:5 NIV

This verse isn't about durable batteries; it isn't about a tough truck, and it isn't discussing the endurance that a cross country athlete requires. This kind of enduring is about love and goodness that is so ingrained in an eternal being that it never, never goes away. Living in eternity is difficult to fathom. For those who love to know the answers and find their security in certainty, the idea of forever can be overwhelming.

Think about this: would you enjoy hanging out with your family and your best buddies forever? What would it be like to have before you an endless summer of being at the beach, golfing, playing tennis, and reading? It would be amazing! It's what we aim for in retirement. We want this season of respite as well as purpose in our lives. It is why we work so hard early on in life—so we can enjoy the final, hopefully quieter years at the end. Ha! The joke is on us! God, in his enduring love and faithfulness, has already prepared our retirement in heaven.

What would you be excited to do forever, not necessarily endlessly, but not having to stop if you didn't want to?

ANSWER TO PATIENCE

Better to be patient than powerful;
better to have self-control than to conquer a city.

PROVERBS 16:32 NLT

In context of the larger chapter, this verse is really about committing your path to God and following his direction with patience and self-control. But humanity does not do well with those virtues. We have seen this over and over. Our own irritability rises to the surface when things do not go our way and we lash out at others. What is the answer for us then?

Our answer comes in the form of God's Spirit who was sent to be our helper. The Holy Spirit is our counselor and guide. When we trust him, we can have the patience we need to do his will. You have likely known the closeness and kindness of his guidance to lead you to where you are today. Commit your way to him and ask today to be filled with his Spirit again.

How can you put your will aside and seek his today?

SPLENDID

Splendid and majestic is His work,
And His righteousness endures forever.

PSALM 111:3 NASB

You may think of a sugar substitute when you read
the word *splendid*, but it means excellent, magnificent,
luxurious, grand, elegant, or stylish. When we consider its
meaning, it may bring to mind a hotel that few can afford to
stay in, or a car that only the rich can drive, or a large house
overlooking a cliff that movie stars call home. Basically, as
an adjective, few can afford the splendid things in this life.

That is what is so great about God! He is splendid. He is
magnificent. He is grand. He is available to everyone. We
have a Father who gives good gifts, is generous, and loves
us. We have an inheritance that we cannot comprehend; it
is glorious beyond our imagination. It is splendid, and it
will be ours to enjoy one day.

*What in your life, apart from your possessions and your
status, is splendid? Does your heart comprehend the work of
God as splendid?*

TRUE NOURISHMENT

"My flesh is true food, and my blood is true drink.
Anyone who eats my flesh and drinks my blood
remains in me, and I in him."

JOHN 6:55-56 NLT

Our true nourishment comes from receiving Jesus
spiritually; he refers to himself as the Bread of Life. By
receiving him, we receive eternal life. His blood is the new
covenant with us. We have communion with other believers
as a reminder of this covenant and the forgiveness of our
sins. This new covenant was made with an eternal sacrifice:
the shedding of Jesus' blood which washed away our sins.

This type of faith is a daily exercise in spiritual discipleship
and discipline. It is our belief in these truths which provides
us with everlasting life. As you read his Word today, feel
his strength filling you for the journey ahead. Know that he
watches over you and cares about you.

*As you go about your day, how can you be aware of God's
activity and therefore acknowledge his strength?*

REMAINING STUDIOUS

Continue in what you have learned and have become convinced of, because you know those from whom you learned it, and how from infancy you have known the Holy Scriptures, which are able to make you wise for salvation through faith in Christ Jesus.

2 TIMOTHY 3:14-15 NIV

The Bible is full of commendations for those who are focused on learning. It promotes wisdom, security, understanding, and preparedness. When you consider people who are geniuses and read about their lives, a constant for them was the practice of learning. To that point, a philosopher and scientist said that the more he learns, the more he realizes how much he doesn't know. That humility should be what we experience as we learn.

There is a warning, however, that knowledge without humility can bring about pride. Many well-educated people deny God based on their skewed understanding of their own knowledge. It is important in our studies to remain humble and to show openness to the Spirit of God and allow him to speak through others. Be encouraged to read more and invite others into your study, especially as it relates to God.

What intrigues you about God and his nature? What can you learn today that will increase your faith in Christ Jesus?

RUNNING ON EMPTY

He who supplies seed to the sower and bread for food will also supply and increase your store of seed and will enlarge the harvest of your righteousness.

2 CORINTHIANS 9:10 NIV

The journey of leadership can be lonely at times. We may even feel like we are running on empty many of our days. If this is the case, we likely need to find a restful place and take some time to ourselves. But when we cannot take the time to rejuvenate and life just keeps coming at us, we can look to our provider who gives us both the seeds to grow and the food to eat. It is a double provision that will strengthen us and bless the work of our hands.

When you are in that stressful place and the walls seem to be closing in, look to your Father in heaven. He promises to be the lifter of your head and the provider for all your needs. He knows what you need before you even ask.

What do you need in your daily life to remind you that God is your provider?

March

Don't worry because I am with you.
"Don't be afraid, because I am your God.
I will make you strong and will help you;
I will support you with my right hand that saves you."

Isaiah 41:10 ncv

SAY IT BETTER

Stay alert! Watch out for your great enemy, the devil.
He prowls around like a roaring lion,
looking for someone to devour.

1 PETER 5:8 NLT

What is it about drama? It seems that people love to feed off the stories of others making mistakes or being unkind to one another. Gossip is the enemy's misinformation tactic, and unfortunately it often works really well on us. We fall hard for a good story about someone's failures; it's unkind but we feel better about ourselves when we are not the one failing.

But kudos to those who can walk away when an unedifying conversation starts, or better yet, who can stop gossip in its tracks. The best method of turning gossip into grace is to say something positive about the person who is the target of the negative words. When we speak either about something we are thankful for or something compassionate, it upends the negative. Guard yourself and others against this roaring lion that devours us so easily. You can inspire change in this regard through your leadership.

How does a positive word about another person make you feel? Can you encourage someone today?

PRODUCE THE ENVIRONMENT

Always be humble, gentle, and patient, accepting each other
in love. You are joined together with peace through the
Spirit, so make every effort to continue together in this way.

EPHESIANS 4:2-3 NCV

This is a tough one when we consider who we are as we lead
others in any position of authority. Most accomplishments
are built on some measurement of gains or progress.
We look at productivity or growing interest in a certain
product. Accomplishments are earned through enduring
excellence in production and consistent refinement of goals
and measures. And naturally, a work environment does
not usually stimulate natural grace or patience. Making
allowance for failure is not an option, and high-performing
members are rewarded.

The problem then, is showing Christ-like behavior in a
world that does not value it. For the drivers of productivity,
this is especially tough. If that's you, it likely weighs heavily
on you. Just to be clear, God is not expecting you to
produce an environment like church in the secular world,
but he trusts all of us to represent him well as we tactfully
engage with society. He will give you strength and grace
because he is patient and loving. Trust in him and let his
peace flow out of you toward others.

*How can you build trust in God so his peace fills your heart
and flows out of you?*

LIFE IS SHORT

"LORD, remind me how brief my time on earth will be.
Remind me that my days are numbered
how fleeting my life is."

PSALM 39:4 NLT

Life is short, but goodness—sometimes it seems the tough times last too long! Throughout our life journeys we have a few permanent fixtures that anchor us. One is God. Another is change. Both are undeniably active. One creates consistent, lasting stability and love. The other keeps us on our toes. It is important to recognize both in this brief time on earth.

We can allow God to anchor us in the middle of change, or we can fight change and try to anchor ourselves. The latter option is an impossible task that creates an embittered individual who is angry at whatever life inflicts upon them. The former option, however, is the key to our success as Christians. As we look to God and allow him to strengthen us, he helps us with change. The secret is to dwell upon his promises, eagerly await our own resurrections, and seek the Holy Spirit. This will ensure our eternal destiny in his everlasting kingdom!

What is permanent in your life? What do you regularly put your trust in?

NECESSARY POLITENESS

Remind them to never tear down anyone with their words or quarrel, but instead be considerate, humble, and courteous to everyone.

TITUS 3:2 TPT

In your job do you calculate potential energy using mass, gravity, and height? If not, do you remember learning that in school? Few of us do. But we know what it means to be civil and to consider others. We do remember the lessons we had as children in how to be polite. Why? Because we encounter the necessity for it every day. Additionally, anything tied to emotion—for example, having any human interaction—makes it much easier to recall because our memories and our emotions function from the same region of the brain.

Being polite is something God favors over being discourteous or argumentative. He wants us to represent him in the way we act and speak. In our hurried lives or when we are just annoyed, we can tend toward speaking or acting in a cold or even rude manner. Sometimes it seems that a detached demeanor comes with the territory of leadership. But we can change this by going back to the basics, slowing ourselves down, and treating people—no matter who they are—with respect.

In those times when you are agitated, how can you remind yourself to slow down and demonstrate civility and kindness?

TRULY EXCEPTIONAL

"Many women have done excellently,
but you surpass them all."

PROVERBS 31:29 ESV

When helping people to write their resumé it is necessary to point out that writers should not add too many superfluous adjectives. People do tend to overstate their own abilities and potential employers are well aware of this. It is difficult to be truly exceptional because everyone thinks they are! In school, students receive awards for special work, extraordinary effort, and remarkable performance. But these seem to be handed out so flippantly that we have lost the meaning of "exceptional." What does it mean to be truly brilliant and to display incomparable skill at a task? We are talking about humans who are the tops of their fields: Nobel Prize winners, Olympic medalists, and other amazing achievers.

If he were on earth today, Jesus would be at the top of the list when it comes to his outstanding persona and performance. He was astonishingly wise, extremely loving, and amazingly unique. His same Spirit dwells in you today and you can rely on him to help you lead at an excellent standard.

How has Christ made you a better leader?

PRINCIPLED

When they hurled their insults at him, he did not retaliate;
when he suffered, he made no threats. Instead, he entrusted
himself to him who judges justly.

1 PETER 2:23 NIV

If you have been to Italy, you have probably observed
some amazing, centuries old architecture. There are many
impressive pieces to view, buried remains of civilizations
brought to life through careful excavation. But some
edifices stand out more than others. Structures like Trajan's
Column stand at nearly a hundred feet tall after a couple of
millennia of battles, storms, and earthquakes.

Principled people are like Trajan's Column. They stand
sturdily, and sometimes alone, through the storms and
battles that rage around them. They remain resolute
throughout the battering and the tribulations. Their
laurels are earned because of a foundation that cannot be
shaken. Their hearts are secure in what they know. Like
Christ, though they have faced assaults and demeaning
circumstances, they trust in the one who judges fairly and
will make all things right.

*Standing out in a wicked generation is not easy. What helps
you stay the course and remain a principled witness for God?*

Unlimited

His divine power has granted to us everything pertaining to
life and godliness, through the true knowledge of Him who
called us by His own glory and excellence.

2 PETER 1:3 NASB

God's power is enough to sustain us and to promote
godliness in our lives. He does not seem to have a limit on
what he provides, but we are limited in what we can receive.
Our limits mostly relate to our ability to take him at his
word. Much like Jesus was limited to perform miracles in
the places where there was unbelief, God limits himself by
our doubts and unbelief.

However, through the true knowledge of him, we are able to
obtain all we need to live a godly life. The starting place for
casting aside doubt is to be consistently reading his Word
and studying his character. Once we know the person of God
behind the Words, we will grow in our faith with all that he
has to say to his followers. He is faithful, just, loving, and
patient. If we can start with those characteristics as a premise,
reading his Word and doing what he says will be easier.

*What are the characteristics about God that you seek and
value?*

RUTHLESS SELF-INTEREST

Do not let my heart incline to any evil,
to busy myself with wicked deeds
in company with men who work iniquity,
and let me not eat of their delicacies!

PSALM 141:4 ESV

Our world is emotionally and spiritually carnivorous, meaning that people are generally marked by ruthless self-interest. It's a dog-eat-dog world. As humans, we have learned how to further ourselves and make our lives easier, but the cost has been significant. We use each other to get ahead, and chase after wealth at the cost of real relationships. We pursue the iridescent item, the power person, and the fabulous fashion more than a healthy connection with our Creator. This is the downfall of our sin nature.

Our selfish pursuits push us away from God and back into ourselves. But thank Jesus that he came and delivered us! He set us free from the daily grind that binds us to our sins. Because of him, we will rise as new creations and live for eternity, liberated from the inclinations of evil. What a sweet promise we have because of Christ!

How can you set your eyes on God and stay fixed on him more than on the selfish desires that distract you away from him?

PRAYERFUL SPIRIT

Rejoice always, pray without ceasing, in everything give thanks; for this is the will of God for you in Christ Jesus.

1 THESSALONIANS 5:16-18 NASB

Have you ever been able to do something without being interrupted all day? Not likely. When Paul wrote to pray without ceasing, if he truly meant it literally, how would you get anything done? We know for a fact that Paul did much more than just pray all the time. He was a traveling missionary who mostly supported himself by working in each place he went. Often, he would have discussions at synagogues and with city elders. He could stop doing life to pray, and neither is that his intention in today's verse.

So, what did he mean? Paul was admonishing us to live in a Spirit of prayer and conversations with God. He instructed us to walk as though Christ is walking next to us and we are sharing our lives with him constantly. When our very thoughts are conversations with the Father, all of sudden we become walking prayers. That is what it means to be a truly prayerful person.

How can you incorporate unceasing prayer into your daily living?

HELD CAPTIVE

His light broke through the darkness and
he led us out in freedom from death's dark shadow
and snapped every one of our chains.

PSALM 107:14 TPT

Have you ever been held captive against your will? It doesn't just happen in prison. Kids sometimes experience this in a classroom. Adults can experience it at work. We look distractedly out the window, and we're not engaged with what is going on around us. We see the weather report in the morning, and we think about outdoor activities the rest of the day. From the time we arrive at our destination in the morning until the moment we leave at the end of the day, anticipation has been building. The bell tolls or the clock strikes, and there is immediate liberation! Though it's just a small dose of what true captivity is like, it is a great feeling to be free to go and do whatever we want.

When we take time to think about the resurrection, we look forward to the day when we will have no more stress, pain, fear, anxiety, or sin. Our burdens will be lifted, and we will be filled with peace, goodness, joy, and righteousness. That will be the most amazing liberation!

What excites you most about entering eternity?

You Are Needed

Some parts of the body that seem weakest and least important are actually the most necessary... So, God has put the body together such that extra honor and care are given to those parts that have less dignity. This makes for harmony among the members, so that all the members care for each other.

1 Corinthians 12:22, 24-25 nlt

God's level of inclusiveness is exclusive. It is astounding that he can take all parts of society and all people groups, and make them unified, cooperative, and functional. It is a societal miracle. It may be one of the greatest miracles outside of the incarnation and the resurrection. And in that worldwide melting pot is you.

You are needed. You are wanted by God for his purposes. You have a contribution to make to his kingdom plan, and he has placed in you the skills, gifts, and talents that are unique to you. He gave you a role in leadership so you can guide others and help bring people together. What you do is important to him, and he will give you the temperance and endurance for your specific task.

What are some of your greatest assets? How can they be used for God's plan to bring people closer to him?

ALL BEAUTY

He has made everything beautiful in its time.
He has also set eternity in the human heart;
yet no one can fathom what God has done
from beginning to end.

ECCLESIASTES 3:11 NIV

Beauty captivates us. Just sit and watch others when
an attractive person walks by. But beauty is not only in
people; we see, hear, taste, and feel a lot of creation that
is amazingly lovely. Think of strong granite mountains
cascading with water down jagged cliffs and through green
canopies. Or listen to a musical marvel in an orchestra
hall as the musicians create exquisite notes that pull you
through the story of their song. Or taste an amazing meal
comprised of the best meats, vegetables, and spices, all
creating a salivation celebration. The luxury of touch is so
satisfying as we grip new leather on a steering wheel, touch
smooth silk, or feel refreshingly cold water on our skin on
a hot day.

Many things around us are beautiful, and we only need to
pause a moment to see, hear, taste, or feel them. And who
created all this splendor? God. His promise is for more
than we now experience, and his eternity with its awesome
pleasures will last forever!

*Take a moment today to experience what beauty God has
placed around you, and in the people you work with.*

REFINED FOR PURITY

These troubles come to prove that your faith is pure. This
purity of faith is worth more than gold, which can be
proved to be pure by fire but will ruin. But the purity of
your faith will bring you praise and glory and honor when
Jesus Christ is shown to you.

1 PETER 1:7 NCV

Gold and precious metals are still refined by fire today as
they have always been because the process of purification
and molding requires extreme heat. What does that look
like in a believer? Must we go through tremendous trials
to prove our faith? For those of us not living in extreme
poverty or volatility of some kind such as war, pestilence,
natural disaster, we have few trials that truly test us
physically. We are tested, however, in the areas of idolatry,
passivity, and social responses. Do we speak as Christ
would in a perverse generation? Do we live as Christ would,
or are we indistinguishable from the rest of the planet's
dwellers?

Purity requires refinement, and that develops in us as we
subject ourselves to listening to and obeying the Holy
Spirit, not just through traumatic circumstances, but
through obedience in our daily decisions. We choose to
pick up our crosses and follow Christ.

What are some significant ways in which you imitate Christ?

What and When

Every good gift and every perfect gift is from above, coming down from the Father of lights, with whom there is no variation or shadow due to change.

JAMES 1:17 ESV

The Father of lights is upright. There is no evil in him. He is consistent and does not waver in the face of humanity. Nothing can stand against him, and no one is beyond his reach. He is good, just, and loving. He is God. In consideration of these facts, it is easy to understand why he gives good gifts which are perfect and specific for each individual. He wouldn't give anything that would cause us to stray, nor would he hold anything back from us so that we would struggle unnecessarily.

God's knowledge of exactly what we need and when we need it is precise. He is not limited by the physical world; all that is created has come from him. He simply spoke everything into being. Why would he not have the ability to provide all that we need? Why would we ever doubt him?

Can you see the bounty in your life which God has provided? Take some time to thank him for his many blessings.

Synchronized

> I have no greater joy than to hear that my children are walking in the truth.

3 John 1:4 esv

When we think about the people we serve as leaders, one of our greatest joys is the knowledge that people are pleased to work in their respective roles. It is critical that each person understands their own limitations, abilities, and traits, and they are able to use them to fulfill their respective roles. Knowing themselves and being true to who they are creates an authentic work environment. We want people who can be aligned in themselves and to their talents, as it helps them to be confident in accomplishing what they set out to do.

You have an important role in providing a healthy environment which will help those with whom you work. Sometimes tough conversations are necessary, but ultimately, they provide the most fruitful outcomes. The encouragement from this is to continue to serve as a willing leader and help create competent members who are enjoyably productive!

If you applied energy and focus to your team, what would change in their productivity levels?

It Takes a While

I consider everything a loss because of the surpassing worth of knowing Christ Jesus my Lord, for whose sake I have lost all things. I consider them garbage, that I may gain Christ.

PHILIPPIANS 3:8 NIV

How do we attribute value to something? For instance, why do we value gold over iron ore? Why are diamonds cherished more than pebbles? Is it not because of its scarcity or the work involved in obtaining it? We place importance, distinction, and value on things that merit them. God says that he keeps himself hidden so that only those who seek him will find him. Like gold and diamonds, it takes work to build a relationship with God, not because he wants to play hard to get, but because he wants us to value what we find and to treat that relationship as precious.

When we discover something too easily, it can be discarded too quickly. Remember that God says that those who are drawn to him will be kept ever closer as they keep seeking him. Your pursuit of him will be rewarded both in eternity as well as in your ever-growing desire to know him.

In your life, what truly has merit?

CHEAP ALTERNATIVES

Delight yourself in the LORD,
and he will give you the desires of your heart.

PSALM 37:4 ESV

The saying "you are what you eat," when you think about it, seems rather gross. Perhaps you traveled in Asia and ate fried chicken feet, balut, or raw seaweed with mushy fish and noodles. Aside from being adventuresome with your palate, what are you? When the phrase is not taken literally, it simply implies that if you eat good food, you will be healthier and feel better. If you eat foods that are unhealthy, you will be unhealthy.

There is a correlation from this statement to today's verse and it's related to our spiritual lives. When we delight in something, we pursue it. We consume it. We want it. God created us to enjoy good things, but for all of the good he made, there are cheap and evil alternatives. They are also enjoyable; they're just not good for you. When you are delighting in God, those desires of your heart for more righteousness are from him. Think of Romans 8; when you live in accordance with the Spirit, you desire the things of the Spirit.

How can you inspire a greater pursuit of God's Spirit in yourself and in others?

Transformed and Renewed

Do not be conformed to this world, but be transformed by the renewing of your mind, so that you may prove what the will of God is, that which is good and acceptable and perfect.

ROMANS 12:2 NASB

The young man had begun experimenting with drugs as a twelve-year-old. His addiction slowly grew to the point that, before his senior year was completed, he abandoned his home and his schooling. His brain was fried, but he only cared about the next high. In one magnificent moment, however, God changed his life forever. While he was in a drug-induced trance, an angel came to visit him. He was so afraid that he cried out to God. His high, and his addiction, ceased to exist. His eyes were opened immediately, and he was filled with a hunger to read the Word of God. As he did so, his brain healed; old connections which had been destroyed by the drugs, were renewed. He became a walking Bible reference and eventually he learned and grew enough to be a teacher and lecturer for the Lord.

God is not limited by anything physical, emotional, or spiritual. He can renew any of us. Can he rehabilitate even the darkest of minds? Yes, he can. Our transformation and renewal are part of what God can and will do in us.

Can you see how God has renewed your mind over the time you have been a believer?

Hypothermia

Remember to welcome strangers, because some who have done this have welcomed angels without knowing it.

HEBREWS 13:2 NCV

Imagine a life filled with sadness, despair, violence, and trouble. That life gives a person true hypothermia of the soul. They become cold and calloused, and for some it can even lead to death. It is why Jesus was so warm to those who lived through trauma. He didn't judge them and push them away; he drew them in. He was the warmth they needed.

Sometimes we see brokenness of the soul as edgy and resistant, but God can see through that. He willingly died for us even while we were sinners and unknowingly resistant to him. As we take on his image and his heart, we can reflect his character to others as well. We can welcome the stranger with a smile. And when the hurt and broken are seeking God and they meet us, they will feel his warmth and peace.

What about your leadership helps others feel included?

FAITH ALONE

"Because he loves me," says the LORD,"I will rescue him;
I will protect him, for he acknowledges my name.
He will call upon me, and I will answer him."

PSALM 91:14-15 NIV

Our love for God is paramount to our faith. When asked
what the greatest commandment was, it rolled off Jesus'
tongue: that we love God and others as we love ourselves.
There was no pondering by Jesus. We know that the need
for this sacrificial love is true in our lives, and we desire
to love God more, but it is not easy in a world of everyday
busyness and the mounting need for more. Things that
trouble us regularly, especially sin, keep us from the
devotion and purity that we want with God. Our good
desires and deeds will never be enough, so what do we do?

We rely on Jesus, the author and finisher of our faith. He
endured, he suffered, and he was punished for our sins.
It is our faith in him alone that keeps us on the right path
toward him and eternity. Keep placing all of your faith and
hope in the salvation and resurrection of Jesus Christ.

How can you ensure Jesus remains your focus?

CELEBRATED

Celebrate with praises the God and Father of our Lord Jesus
Christ, who has shown us his extravagant mercy. For his
fountain of mercy has given us a new life—we are reborn to
experience a living, energetic hope through the resurrection
of Jesus Christ from the dead.

1 PETER 1:3 TPT

March is the month we celebrate the beginning of spring
in the northern hemisphere. It is a time of new life, new
beginnings, and fresh creativity. In this season, it feels good
to be alive especially if you have been locked away and
limited during the frigid winter.

Whether it's the start of spring, a new life, or the end of a
cold winter, celebration is done best with others. That is
the greatest way to enjoy what has occurred or is about to
occur. It reminds us of our created purpose to enjoy all that
God has blessed us with. When we exult in our liberation
from eternal death and remember the freedom we have
because of Christ's sacrifice, we receive energetic hope for a
future of living out God's plans for us.

*What can you do to encourage celebration with praises in
your group of friends?*

COHERENT

"This people's heart has become calloused;
they hardly hear with their ears,
and they have closed their eyes.
Otherwise, they might see with their eyes,
hear with their ears,
understand with their hearts
and turn, and I would heal them."

MATTHEW 13:15 NIV

Have you ever had one of those days when it seems that everything you say or do is taken the wrong way? You try to lead by example, speak coherently, and connect to people, but everyone misunderstands. Jesus had days like that. He spoke clearly to his disciples about his coming kingdom and his future reign. They did not understand. Part of the reason was because for four hundred years, they had been waiting for a warrior savior. Jesus fit the bill (except for the warrior part), but they did not understand what he was saying.

We are in a different place and time. Because of God's mercy, we come to Jesus as readers and listeners of the Bible. We read his Word and we long to understand him. We want him to reveal himself to us so we can know him and follow him fully. And we can trust that he is faithful to teach his followers. We will hear from him.

How can you practice listening to God?

THE KEY

Through him we have also obtained access by faith
into this grace in which we stand,
and we rejoice in hope of the glory of God.

ROMANS 5:2 ESV

Faith is the key to Christianity. A key unlocks a door and gives rights to whatever is inside. Faith allows for salvation and gives us access to all that God has for us. Without it, we do not have access to God's promises. Without it, we do good works and thereby attempt to gain our own salvation. And without faith, our continuous sanctification cannot take place. It is imperative then that we foster faith in ourselves and our communities.

How do we build faith? First, faith is a gift from God, so we pray for him to grow it within us. Second, we can share godly lives with other believers, encourage one another in our experiences with him, and spend time together in his Word and in praise and worship. As we do these things, we increasingly recognize his involvement in our lives. We begin to build trust in his character and have more assurance that he is actively working alongside us. As overseers, we are provided the opportunity to encourage faith in one another and encouragement in God.

What can you do to display faith in your workplace?

Taking a Seat

The Son is the radiance of God's glory and the exact
representation of his being, sustaining all things by his
powerful word. After he had provided purification for sins,
he sat down at the right hand of the Majesty in heaven. So
he became as much superior to the angels as the name he
has inherited is superior to theirs.

Hebrews 1:3-4 niv

This isn't just about Jesus accomplishing a task and taking
a seat to review what he completed. This is about the praise
and honor given to Jesus as the Son of God.

Sitting down at the right hand of the Father acknowledges
his authority and position in creation. We are reminded
of Jesus' power; that by his Word he can speak and what
he says is complete. He is no longer constrained by his
humanity but as the first of the resurrected and as fully God
and fully man, he is exalted on high. No one compares to
him, and all of creation answers to him. What a great Savior
we have!

What do you love about Jesus? How can you praise him today?

FAITHFUL EXAMPLE

Let no one despise you for your youth, but set the believers
an example in speech, in conduct, in love, in faith, in purity.

1 TIMOTHY 4:12 ESV

Being above reproach, outstanding in example, or
tenaciously pure in conduct is impossible. Sorry if that
bursts any bubbles, but it is the truth. We are broken
vessels, and we need fixing. We require salvation. We
require a different spirit. We require consistent help. The
best place for us to start is with humility.

Being humble is not an opportunity to make excuses for
failing as leaders, or to require others to pour out more
grace on our behalf. We do not say we are sinners as a
reason to keep sinning. We know this, and in humility, and
with a contrite heart we approach the throne of grace. We
serve a holy God who is worthy of honor and glory. So,
our purpose in leadership is to be an example for others to
follow with meekness and gentleness. In the same manner
with which we are loved, forgiven, and accepted by God,
we, too, choose to love, forgive, and accept others. This is
how we will faithfully exemplify the person of Christ.

*How can you continue to practice humility in the presence of
those you serve?*

DEPENDABLE COMPANION

Some trust in chariots and some in horses,
but we trust in the name of the LORD our God.

PSALM 20:7 NIV

To get to where we are in leadership, we have had to make some tough decisions. It comes with the territory. Being decisive is important as a leader. When we waver or show uncertainty it affects those who look to us for our authority. This can be discouraging to people. Awareness of this tendency places a weight on us to be informed, strategic, and observant of critical issues that may need addressing. To do this well, we have to rely on others. We cannot sustain a full picture when we're isolated, nor can we endure the weight of responsibility without support.

When we are alone in leadership, we tend to become reactive. Indecision can lead to impulsive behavior, and that is the antithesis of good management. Every person feels alone sometimes, so it is critical for us to ensure that we are connected with a faithful person. That person is our Savior and faithful friend, Jesus. He will give us what we need. This is not to dismiss the importance of other people in our lives, but in times when we are unaccompanied, he will be our dependable companion and our perfect example.

How can you draw closer to Jesus when you feel alone?

INSPIRATION FROM WHERE

"He has filled him with the Spirit of God, with wisdom, with understanding, with knowledge and with all kinds of skills—to make artistic designs for work in gold, silver and bronze."

EXODUS 35:31-32 NIV

What inspires you? Does your inspiration get you out of bed in the morning? How often do you find yourself drifting off and thinking about whatever fuels you or daydreaming while in a meeting? Inspiration takes place when we make space for it. It is an important aspect in the life of humans as it pairs naturally with creativity. We were made to create. What is beautiful about mankind is that our inspiration varies. Our creative inspiration occurs in very broad spheres which makes for so much of the beauty around us.

We can get busy with life. Time is taken up in our responsibilities: a job, a spouse, a family, a home, studying, volunteering, or spending time with friends. It can stifle inspiration if we don't leave time and space for it. And when we are not stimulated by new thoughts or envisioning new things, we can feel stuck in a repetitive circle. How do we break out of routine to find inspiration when we fill our lives with busyness?

What can you say no to today that will give you room for inspiration?

AUTHENTIC LEADERS

I resolved to know nothing while I was with you except
Jesus Christ and him crucified. I came to you in weakness
and fear, and with much trembling.

1 CORINTHIANS 2:2-3 NIV

A new wave has crashed our society and has caused a major
change. This generation is not looking for leaders who are
experts or who have it all together. They want leaders who
are authentic. It is hard for leaders who were trained for
generations to demonstrate other traits: learning, self-
control, and authority. But so much failure in past leaders
has led to a generation crying out for authenticity. They
want to see our mistakes and to learn from them. They
want to work with us and learn with us, so we are inspired
together. It is a shift that enables more transparency, but
it has also loosened morality. We are broken people, and
human leadership is doomed to failure.

Jesus is authentic. He is sincere, realistic, trustworthy,
faithful, and dependable. We sharpen who we are by
following Jesus' example and by living in the same manner
as he lived. Jesus was not ashamed because he lived as
himself, and his leadership was genuine. We don't need
another leader to fail. In any case, no man should be exalted
that much. We need Jesus. His leadership is perfect.

What aspects of authenticity do you value?

CAPABLE

"There are many workmen with you, stonecutters, masons of stone, and carpenters, and all of them are skillful in every kind of work. Of the gold, silver, bronze, and iron there is no limit. Arise and work, and may the LORD be with you."

1 CHRONICLES 22:15-16 NASB

It is refreshing to find someone to whom you can hand a project or a job to and know that they will proficiently complete it. These people are the twenty percent of the population that do eighty percent of the work. They are skilled, adept, and accomplished, and much of it has to do with how they apply themselves in their daily lives. These are diligent people who are not complacent about their learning. They continue to develop new skills, and they perform those skills with competence. They are the ones who get promoted, gain the attention of their leaders, and are admired for their hard work.

As leaders, we provide vision, guide the execution of that vision, and deliver the final results of a project. To do this, we need to stay contemporary, be consistent in our characters, and communicate clearly with everyone. We hear God his people call to arise and work, and we answer that call willingly.

What new skill can you learn that will enable greater capabilities within yourself or those you lead?

AWESOME POWER

Let us be grateful for receiving a kingdom that cannot be shaken, and thus let us offer to God acceptable worship, with reverence and awe.

HEBREWS 12:28 ESV

Imagine holding enough power to speak a word and immediately something is created. Just by thinking of something, you can bring it to life. What has taken us years to build or perhaps a lifetime to create, can instead be made from just a few words. If something is against us, we can speak, and it is immediately destroyed. That is awe-inspiring power. What would it be like if you held that power? What reverence would people have for you? You would be famous. People would worship you and proclaim that you are the great one.

This is the power our God has. He has unlimited knowledge and wisdom. He has justice, mercy, and love. His authority is wielded with such great wisdom; it is awe inspiring. How great is our God! Let us be still and be in awe of his majesty.

As you reflect today on God's splendor, what in creation demonstrates his power to you?

THE ANTAGONIST

Have mercy on me, O God,
because of your unfailing love.
Because of your great compassion,
blot out the stain of my sins.

PSALM 51:1 NLT

The boy cried out, "Mercy!" After being released, he shook
his arm and tried to loosen his shoulder while glaring at
his brother. "Why did you do that so hard?" What he really
wanted to do was punch him in the face, but he knew that
such provocation would receive no clemency. After all,
he deserved some form of punishment because he kept
taunting his brother. There was, initially, some forbearance,
but after he poked his brother in the head the fourth time,
he aroused the beast and was set upon. This was a normal
day between the two. The antagonist worked until he
started to receive his just reward, and then interrupted it by
crying out for compassion.

In this story, we are the antagonists. We go about our days
repeating similar mistakes, and even worse, repeating the
sins that so easily entangle us. We have but one retort,
"Mercy!" We are wretched individuals standing before a
holy God. We deserve great punishment yet, when we cry
out for mercy, he looks at us with love, and remembers his
sacrifice. Our sins are forgiven, and we receive mercy from
our benevolent God.

Do you demonstrate mercy to those who offend you?

APRIL

I can do all things through Christ,
because he gives me strength.

PHILIPPIANS 4:13 NCV

LASER FOCUS

Turn my eyes from looking at worthless things;
and give me life in your ways.

PSALM 119:37 ESV

They say that when someone is at the top of their game, they have laser focus. People with this level of attention set aside distractions and no matter what their role— athlete, actor, employee, owner or other—the attentive and diligently industrious come out on top. There is no secret to success. There is no quick fix; it just takes patient concentration to see something through to its fruition. But allow your eyes to be cast aside to fruitless endeavors, whether it is sin or simply wasting time with entertainment of some sort, and you will not be rewarded.

When we take our eyes off the prize, we rarely achieve our goals by chance. There are countless examples of this in our lives as well as in Scripture. As the saying goes, *you cannot hit what you do not aim at*. You are building into your life, with consistent target practice, the ability to focus on Jesus and his Word. You will hit the mark and become more like him because of your practiced faithfulness. He promises to reward your diligence.

Why does God want your mind engaged in his Word and in prayer?

ONE SMALL ACT

"I, Nebuchadnezzar, praise and exalt and glorify the King of heaven, because everything he does is right and all his ways are just. And those who walk in pride he is able to humble."

DANIEL 4:37 NIV

Having no dignity, the man openly urinated in the street, unaware of people walking by. His coat was torn, his hair was matted, and his head sported a tilted cap. He didn't care. But not long ago he was a different man. Four years earlier he was a top executive, controlling interests across the world and working in his office on the upper floors of the very building where he was urinating. It was the anniversary of his departure and he wanted to make his mark. As he drunkenly fumbled with his zipper, he wondered how he had crashed so hard. Losing his wife was hurtful, but the shame of falling so far from the top echelons of the corporate world was disgraceful.

It all started with one small act of deceit. One dishonorable act led to another. He turned, regretting his past choices. Previously he was a distinguished man exalted by his peers, and now he was a vagabond. Thinking about it more, he realized he lost his way when he was impressed by his own success. He no longer acknowledged the God who made him and gave him his honorable title.

How can you intentionally honor God in your life?

EVEN THE BEST

The prayer of a righteous person is powerful and effective.

JAMES 5:16 NIV

Our righteousness is dependent on Jesus Christ alone. We know we are all sinners and that there is no person who can call themselves righteous. Even the best of us cannot stand before God. Therefore, our prayer life has to start with humility and a position of dependence upon God. We can also begin with an attitude of gratitude because Jesus Christ took our punishment and provided a way for us to be in fellowship with a holy and righteous God.

Humility, dependence, and gratitude—that is the right combination for God to honor our prayers and to give them his power and effectiveness. He is the activating force behind our prayers, so it should amaze us that he allows us to speak the Word. It is humbling when we begin to understand that he is truly the wind beneath our wings and the breath that gives us voice. Dwell on that today and remind yourself that he who spoke the world into existence is the same person who encourages us to speak his will into this world. That is what we are doing when we pray in humility, dependency, and gratitude.

Ask Jesus what he wants you to pray for today.

MORE EVIDENCE

I am convinced that neither death, nor life, nor angels, nor principalities, nor things present, nor things to come, nor powers, nor height, nor depth, nor any other created thing will be able to separate us from the love of God that is in Christ Jesus our Lord.

ROMANS 8:38-39 NASB

What does it take for us to believe someone is a person of integrity? Do we check their education level, their reputation in the industry, or their political status? Perhaps we just believe people at face value? As we get older it usually takes more evidence to convince us to believe something or someone is truthful. However, Paul, the author of this sentence, was an educated man. He was discipled as a pharisee and raised in Roman society. He was articulate and learned. He knew how to speak and how to dispute arguments. He demonstrated in multiple places throughout his missionary journeys that he was not easily convinced unless there was proof.

When Paul said that he was convinced of something, we should look into it. Who would be confident to contend with a man who could argue well and had the scars to show for it? When it comes to articulating your beliefs, it is the heartfelt and in-depth study of God's Word that will give you confidence in his truth.

How convinced are you in your faith?

WELCOME THE LEAST

"Whoever welcomes this little child in my name welcomes me; and whoever welcomes me welcomes the one who sent me. For it is the one who is least among you all who is the greatest."

LUKE 9:48 NIV

In the business world we read about great people. We study what they have accomplished, and we praise them for their productivity and abilities. We laud those who stand out in their fields as the greatest and the most meaningful in our society. Yet in the upside-down, inside-out kingdom of God, Jesus does not care for those who are at the top of human accomplishments. In fact, most often he resists these people because of their pride.

We know this temptation to be proud all too well ourselves. It feels good to receive praise from men. But we serve a God who does not see things the same ways we do. We should be working together to adopt his mindset and his perspective on our own humanity and what that means in terms of any accomplishment. We want to welcome the least. We want our attention to be on those who require the most help and not on those who feel they have no need of Christ.

Who do you know that is considered lowly and needs help?

DESIRE FOR EXCELLENCE

As you excel in everything—in faith, in speech, in
knowledge, in all earnestness, and in our love for you—
see that you excel in this act of grace also.

2 CORINTHIANS 8:7 ESV

"Meh, that's good enough," is not part of God's vernacular.
He does not ask us to aim for simply satisfactory; he wants
us to aim for excellence. What he makes is excellent;
after all, he made you! We cannot achieve perfection
in our broken world, but if we aim for perfection, we
have a chance of achieving excellence. If we aim to
make something only passable, we will barely achieve a
satisfactory level.

In our daily lives, let's be sure to seek God with an earnest
desire for better-than-average accomplishments. To do so
requires thoughtful meditation and prayer when we take
responsibility for various projects, as well as in our pursuit
of him. How do we find the time, how do we use that
time, and what do we want the results to be? When these
questions are answered they will lead us to improved results
in all our efforts, but especially in our relationship with God.

*How does it feel to know that God created you to be in an
intimate and meaningful relationship with him?*

POSITION OF FAITH

Jesus told his disciples, "If anyone would come after me, let him deny himself and take up his cross and follow me."

MATTHEW 16:24 ESV

We all have in our lives people and assumptions which we believe without questioning them or thinking too much about them. If we are challenged on why we put our faith in gravity, for instance, it is likely we can give some decent explanation which we learned in school. Similarly, if we are asked about why we believe a certain friend is competent and capable, we can deliver a list of proven characteristics to support our faith in that person.

But when we are really pushed about what we believe about God, by his design, it will likely come down to simply a position of faith. Our conclusions can vary depending on arguments for or against. However, when we believe in Jesus, we are certain of our own outcome. We trust what the Word articulates about him. That is what our faith is all about—having conviction in the truth of a matter and living our life in alignment with that truth. Jesus challenges us to lay down everything else and follow him. It is a perilous path that is filled with troubling times and unsettling trials, but we press into him because we believe in the one true God.

Does your life align with what you believe about God?

PERFORMANCE AND PRAISE

You have not received a spirit that makes you fearful slaves.
Instead, you received God's Spirit when he adopted you as
his own children.

ROMANS 8:15 NLT

Have you ever been afraid of someone to whom you are
accountable? Perhaps you feel that in your current role.
Maybe you now face constant scrutiny from those who
oversee your work. If you could say something to them
in your own defense, what would it be? How would you
like them to treat you? What can they do to make you feel
more comfortable while they are still expecting a high
performance out of you?

These questions are tough to think about, but they are
also important. You do not want to feel like a fearful
slave, but neither do those who work for you. As you are
a leader, think about the reversal of those questions and
consider how you can treat those whom you supervise.
What does each of them need to feel less like a slave and
more like a member of the particular group which you
lead? How can you encourage them while still requiring
high performance? What ways can you serve the ultimate
purpose but will also enable those you are responsible for to
function better?

Who needs encouragement among the people you serve?

PEACEFUL RESOLUTION

Through him to reconcile to himself all things, whether on
earth or in heaven, making peace by the blood of his cross.
And you, who once were alienated and hostile in mind,
doing evil deeds, he has now reconciled in his body of flesh
by his death, in order to present you holy and blameless and
above reproach before him.

COLOSSIANS 1:20-22 ESV

Conflict happens. If you have two humans interacting in
any capacity, they will eventually create a scenario in which
one of them is infringed upon by the other. Whether it is an
intended offense or a circumstantial situation, it does not
matter because conflict will ensue.

Each person approaches conflict differently, but studies
demonstrate that there are four responses which are
crushing to relationships—leaving or shutting down,
making the issue unnecessarily large, consistently
seeing each other negatively, and invalidating any
expressed feelings. We will certainly conflict in any
human relationships, but doing so in a healthy manner is
important. Jesus resolved our conflict with God by dying
in our place. He took the hardest road, and though he is
not asking us to do the same, we do need to sacrifice pride
and shame. Our goal should be to imitate Jesus as the
quintessential peacemaker.

*With whom do you currently have a conflict and therefore
also have need of a peaceful resolution?*

Feast on Abundance

They feast on the abundance of your house;
you give them drink from your river of delights.

PSALM 36:8 NIV

Abundant means overflowing, copious, ample, or rich. There is only one who is capable of fulfilling the definition of this word in every aspect. God, the Father, has large quantities of everything possibly necessary to meet our needs. What is intriguing is that he does not require storehouses for his abundance, for he created all things and can meet our needs with a word uttered from his mouth.

Imagine for a moment that you manage an unlimited supply of everything the world needs. Would it be troublesome for you to share this wealth? What if you had a limitless ability to meet these needs? Would there be a limit to your generosity? When you possess literally everything, do you think you'll want more? No. And that is the situation with God. He has everything and he gives in abundance.

Can you stretch out your hand and give to others willingly?

SIMPLY SERVE

"The greatest among you will be your servant."

MATTHEW 23:11 NIV

Of all the things a person can do to humble themselves, understanding the connotations of being a servant must be at the core. A servant simply serves others, but the tasks can range from menial to magnanimous. This posture can be challenging especially for those of us who are given the gift of leadership. It's good to remember, however, that we have a mandate from Jesus to serve those we oversee.

We are never to lord our position over those we lead, but rather we are to care for them while helping them stay focused on our mutual goals and visions. To intentionally subjugate yourself for others in the effort to serve their needs is an act of humility that pleases God. This is the will of God. In our society, there are people in our work and church communities who spend a significant amount of time in service to others. These are the ones we can learn from and emulate. We can aspire to distinguish ourselves as true servants of the Lord by serving in the positions that he has given to us. If you are not there yet, you can start with your family. Practice by simply serving those who are immediately around you in your various responsibilities at work, home, and church.

What do you do to serve others each week?

IT IS COMPLETE

I am sure of this, that he who began a good work in you will bring it to completion at the day of Jesus Christ.

PHILIPPIANS 1:6 ESV

It is that last piece of the puzzle, the report handed in to the boss, the dirt swept off the shop floor after a finished project, and the cool drink on the deck as the sun sets. Ahh, it is complete. There is a feeling of great satisfaction when you finish something you've worked hard on. It can be addictive. Successful people are driven by this feeling; they love to work to completion. If their day ends without it, they may feel dissatisfied.

God is also dissatisfied by incompletion. He will not relent until his work is complete. His goal of dwelling with man in his earthly kingdom will be completed. He is a finisher. You could call it a godly attribute because things left unfinished will not exist in his world. He has ongoing projects as we do. But he will never leave anything he sets his mind to incomplete, and you are part of his work.

What is God working on in you in order to bring to completion his plan for you?

POSITIVE WORKPLACE

"May I find favor in your eyes, my lord," she said. "You have
put me at ease by speaking kindly to your servant."

RUTH 2:13 NIV

Efficiency is usually a healthy element of productivity, but it
can present itself as rude to people. People that are efficient
tend to take less care in how they interact with others, and
instead they favor saving time. The hope is that the less
time they spend talking will result in more time working.
Why have another meeting when an email or a quick chat
will suffice?

This concept is prevalent in the workplace because we
are supposed to be industrious in our society. We want to
make sure that the money we spend on resources—like
people—produces results—like more money! However,
simple kindnesses as one goes zipping through the day will
never go amiss. Asking how someone's day was, offering
to fill their cup, or opening the door for them makes a big
difference in the attitudes of the people on the receiving
end. Positive workplaces are more productive, and you can
help drive that by inspiring your teams to be intentional
in their relationships. It can start with you and how you
engage today with the first person you see.

What ways can you pause to encourage kindness in your team?

EMOTIONAL OUTBURST

Refrain from anger, and forsake wrath!
Fret not yourself; it tends only to evil.

PSALM 37:8 ESV

The businessman was at the point of meltdown. He was supposed to be meeting his wife in another city, and he was running late. Airport check-in and getting through security was slow. He hefted his bags and moved as fast he could toward the gate. When he arrived with sweat dripping down his back, he found the boarding door closing and the jetway pulling back from the plane. He banged angrily on the door as the stress hit him. Lucidity flushed away as he yelled at the door, but it was to no avail. For a few seconds he spouted obscenities as his frustration and overreactive emotions surfaced with no logical reason.

Rationality slowly returned as he calmed down and realized that he had an audience. Shame crept over him. He silently sat and fumed. It is not fun when emotions become unbalanced. We misplace our sensibilities, and rational thinking flies out the window. This is where our good God has given us the Holy Spirit to dwell within us and to aid in self-control and patience. With effort, time, and maturity, emotional outbursts are replaced by logical thinking and consequently, behavior.

In what ways can God help you with self-control?

LEADERSHIP SACRIFICE

When I am afraid,
I put my trust in you.
In God, whose word praise,
in God I trust; I shall not be afraid.
What can flesh do to me?

PSALM 56:3-4 ESV

Most of us do not have leadership bestowed upon us
without a few sacrifices. Hopefully those sacrifices are
not too numerous nor of the type to cause us to become
callous. When we lose faith in humanity, it is difficult to
lead. The best kind of leaders are men and women who can
first learn to follow. They understand humanity from both
perspectives, and their trust is not in one person but in a
corporate body which comes together to complete a vision.

Even better is a leader who knows how to be led by
the Holy Spirit. This person believes in their group or
organization pursuing the same vision and trusting in
Jesus Christ for the processes and the results. As a person
who believes in Jesus even when fear is crouching at the
door, they trust him to overcome the roadblocks and
challenges. There is one person, the man, Jesus Christ, who
will never lack commitment, sacrifice, time, consistency, or
competency. He is a perfect and trustworthy person, and we
can trust that in him we will never fail in his purposes.

How can you build your trust in God?

WHOLESOME LIVING

Taste and see that the LORD is good;
blessed is the one who takes refuge in him.

PSALM 34:8 NIV

Good, healthy bread, for those who can eat it, is amazing.
There's a lot of work ahead of being able to enjoy this type
of bread as it needs to be mixed, kneaded, risen, and baked.
But when a loaf has just come out of the oven, a little butter
on a slice makes for a most wonderful food experience.
Yum. You can never get this same result from manufactured
food. Wholesome food tastes so much better. It satisfies. It
is healthier, tastier, and is usually better for you. But that
result isn't a convenient process, and it always takes that
extra work and investment of time. And it's usually more
expensive; the costs are in time, money, and effort.

Wholesome living is not any different. It will provide
nourishment, better health, and even have a greater taste,
but it is hard work. It is especially hard because there isn't
immediate gratification. And it definitely has a cost; to live
wholesomely you must regularly die to sin and self.

What does nourishing faith look like in the workplace? How
can you encourage it, knowing that it is not a quick process?

CERTIFIED INSPECTION

What then shall we say that Abraham, our forefather according to the flesh, discovered in this matter? If, in fact, Abraham was justified by works, he had something to boast about—but not before God. What does Scripture say? "Abraham believed God, and it was credited to him as righteousness."

ROMANS 4:1-3 NIV

Certified Inspection. This stamp on a document means someone has confirmed its status and it is ready to sell. It has been verified by a professional who confirms that this item is up to standard. "Credited Righteous." This is the stamp on all who believe in Christ, his death, and his resurrection; they follow him as his disciples. This certification is an attribution of righteousness that is not deserved but imputed simply because we believe in Jesus Christ as our redeemer.

When we stand before God and he judges us, he will look at us and say, "This one is forgiven; he is certified righteous!" When all else is stripped away from our lives, what do we have to stand on because of our own work or worth? Nothing. We must rely on what has been credited to us simply by faith in Christ and Christ alone.

Can you throw yourself at the mercy of God? Do you see his kindness every day?

RITE OF PASSAGE

You were called to freedom, brothers. Only do not use your freedom as an opportunity for the flesh, but through love serve one another.

GALATIANS 5:13 ESV

Every year groups of Amish youth leave their homes and communities for Rumspringa, which is the adolescent rite of passage as they experience the world before they decide whether or not they will permanently join the church. Most of them choose to enter the church as full members and remain with their communities. Some, however, choose to leave the church and try the outside experience; things can get wild.

Sometimes the Amish youth go crazy with the liberation in their new lives. They take their freedom and sometimes result in abusing their bodies and hurt themselves and others. Some of them use their liberty for good serving others, traveling the world, doing good for others less fortunate. That is the kind of loving liberty that Paul is encouraging here.

How can you use the freedom you have as a manager to encourage service to one another?

AGAINST THE FLOW

The message of the cross is foolishness to those
who are perishing, but to us who are being saved
it is the power of God.

1 CORINTHIANS 1:18 NKJV

The message of the cross is one of suffering and sacrifice.
Jesus showed us how to live in a way that is averse to
ourselves; being a believer means living in a way that goes
against the natural flow of the human condition. We live for
God's glory.

Jesus' gains were not his own—they belonged to his Father.
When the disciples asked him to show them the Father, he
made it clear his life was not his own. Everything he did
was at the Father's command and for his edification. When
they saw Jesus, they saw the Father. He gave everything of
himself before he arrived at Golgotha, the hill upon which
he was crucified. In our lives today, we sacrifice when we
serve others, or when we fast and pray. This emulates the
sacrifice that Christ made for us. Our sacrifices make firm
steps toward resisting sin in our lives. It also witnesses to
the people around us about Christ living in us and molding
us to be more like him. These are valuable testimonies
before God as he provides his Spirit and his power to equip
us in our pursuit of him.

*What have you given up in your pursuit of worthless things in
order to spend your time, treasures, and talents in seeking God?*

PRONE TO MERCY

Bearing with one another and, if one has a complaint against another, forgiving each other; as the Lord has forgiven you, so you also must forgive.

COLOSSIANS 3:13 ESV

It is painful to hear of lives torn apart by arguments and resistance to mercy. Unfortunately, it is common. God calls us to be a people of peace and to be reconciled to one another. He commands us to forgive those who have sinned against us. He made a way to reconciliation when there was not a way of our own doing by forgiving us for our great sins. Jesus' death brought us reconciliation so that we can find the strength and resilience to be reconciled with others.

When we take time to reflect on our lives, hopefully there is not a situation or a person that we have left unforgiven. If we have, we must take the proper steps to make peace. Sometimes that starts within us or talking with a counselor, and other times we are able to make amends by simply letting a bad memory go. We are stubbornly willing to say no to recalling bad thoughts about anyone. That is what God has done for us by casting our sins as far as the east is from the west. He let it go and so must we.

Who do you need to reconcile with?

INVESTED MANAGER

Jesus declared, "I am the bread of life.
Whoever comes to me will never go hungry,
and whoever believes in me will never be thirsty.

JOHN 6:35 NIV

Jesus was great at speaking to people at their particular level. He knew his audience. To shepherds he spoke of sheep and pastures; to builders he spoke of planning and preparation; to the poor he talked about food and water. His Words were not manipulative. They were impactful because they spoke to the core of what the person was experiencing.

As leaders, we need to be attuned to what our people are working through in a way that is personal and individual, so we can speak into their situations with impact. This doesn't come to the uninvested manager. Like Jesus, we have to make time to understand our audiences and encourage with the right words so that transformation can occur. Change comes when people are driven to take a first step, and that motivation comes from a sense of hope. Like a good shepherd, we want to care for and bring hope to those we lead.

How can you impact your team today with a hopeful message?

WAITING FOR PATIENCE

The Lord is not slow to fulfill his promise as some count slowness, but is patient toward you, not wishing that any should perish, but that all should reach repentance.

2 PETER 3:9 ESV

Patience—how boring! Who has time to wait for patience? Thankfully, the Lord does. His patience for us is necessary because of our propensity toward sin. He is content to work on us slowly, not because we give him anything of value but because Jesus Christ sacrificed himself for us. God's holy judgment is paused and awaiting the right time. For now, we are under his mercy.

Through the work of the Holy Spirit, we see him slowly transforming us and maturing his bride. With this in mind we need to extend mercy with the patience of our God, to our fellow man. There are plenty of opportunities for us to become frustrated by those around us, but a simple reminder of God's goodness and patience for us can delay our anger and frustration for others. May we exemplify the grace and love of our Lord.

How has God's patience with you helped you to extend the same to others?

IN SYNC

Above all these put on love,
which binds everything together in perfect harmony.

COLOSSIANS 3:14 ESV

How often have you seen a group of people in perfect synchronization? Paul encouraged the people of the church at Colossae to take on the mind of Christ, to put aside fleshly behavior, and to live together with all the virtues that only God's Spirit can create in us. Paul commended people to demonstrate compassion, kindness, humility, gentleness, and patience with each other and to those around them. All these traits are to be wrapped up in love and again, this love can only come through the Spirit of God. In that place and with a posture showing these graces, the church will find perfect harmony.

When we ponder this verse, we may have our doubts. Sure, one person may do some of this for a time, but a whole group of people acting like this at the same time? Never. But we have read about God's miracles, and some of us have seen and experienced them. We can never discount the Sprit's ability to do work in us, which is why we continue to strive to get in sync with him.

How can you get in rhythm with God's Spirit? Can you see the changes being forged in your personality?

In All You Do

Whatever you do, in word or deed, do everything in the name of the Lord Jesus, giving thanks to God the Father through him.

COLOSSIANS 3:17 ESV

If we want to get really practical about living a sinless life and honoring God in all we do, this is it. We have to speak all our words and do all our deeds in his name. That should give us pause. If we start by simply praying at the beginning of any word or action, "Jesus, I say and do this in your name," it will cause us to really think.

What things did you do yesterday that would have been different if you did it all in his name? Would you have been less impulsive, have greater control of your thoughts, be more aware of what your body was doing, or become more prayerful? There is no way a person can do this in their own strength. If you start today giving every thought, word, and action to the Lord, imagine the people who will be impacted by you! Imagine if you acted more like Jesus how people would notice because doing things in his name would mean that, more and more, you would behave as he behaved.

If you lived like this, what would change and how would others benefit from it?

TREMBLING WORLD

Be steadfast, immovable, always abounding in the work of the Lord, knowing that in the Lord your labor is not in vain.

1 CORINTHIANS 15:58 ESV

Have you ever been in an earthquake? The whole earth literally shakes. It is terrifying because there is nothing to hold onto that is stable. Everything is moving; nothing is still. What you think is stable can potentially collapse. It is a chaotic experience that no one wants to ever go through. The devastation created by shallow high scale earthquakes is horrific. Often nothing is left standing.

God remains steadfast throughout the worst tragedies and disasters. He is unshakable. His love for us is enduring, and his care for us is resolute. He will not take his eye off us, and though we experience suffering and loss, he is there, always present and ever comforting. His promises will not fail. Though the earth may groan, and the people curse his name, Jesus will return and make all things new. He is our unshakable hope.

How can you continue to do God's work in a condemned and trembling world?

COATTAILS

Do your best to present yourself to God as one approved,
a worker who has no need to be ashamed, rightly handling
the word of truth.

2 TIMOTHY 2:15 ESV

What do we call people who get into study groups to present on a topic, but do not do any of the work? Some people actually think this behavior is smart in some sense, but it is undeniably lazy. Somehow, these people find the groups that have industrious members and manage to ride on that work and effort done by others. We recognize the lazy one and we know they don't deserve the accolades given to the rest of the team.

When we face Jesus, we are encouraged to do more than just rely on what he did for us. Sure, he knocked the presentation out of the park, and it was all him, but God still calls us to emulate what he has done. None of us have merit based on what we do before a holy God. But we can and will be rewarded for pursuing Christ, doing good work, and rightfully handling the Word of God.

What fruit has been born in your life from your pursuit of God?

Childhood Behavior

"Truly I tell you, unless you change and become like little children, you will never enter the kingdom of heaven."

MATTHEW 18:3 NIV

We need to be able to work with people who are competent, capable, and skilled. People who function within an organization or group cannot allow the members to disintegrate into petty squabbles and tantrums. Imagine how quickly things would fall apart if everyone regressed to childhood behavior.

So, what is Jesus saying here? Jesus wants his people to know that the good, sweet, innocent qualities that children inherently possess should stand out to us. Children are eager to learn, open-minded, unpretentious, and have a healthy dependency on others. Jesus is not asking us to regress in our faculties or the maturity levels which we now have. He wants people who believe in him, are not full of themselves, and love others. He wants people who depend on him and are devoted to one another. It is this group of people who will enter into eternity with him.

How can you encourage learning, clear thinking, and healthy dependency in the actions of your team?

GIFTS TO SHARE

Put on then, as God's chosen ones, holy and beloved, compassionate hearts, kindness, humility, meekness, and patience.

COLOSSIANS 3:12 ESV

People praised Jesus for his words. He spoke with authority and clarity. When he was telling a story or a parable, a hush would fall, and people listened intently. They would come up to him later and tell him how amazing he was and how they were engrossed in what he was teaching. His response was simple and humble and always driven by decorum. Jesus would often encourage others in their enthusiasm and willingness to listen and learn. People walked away feeling lighter after being near him and learning from him. They knew they were in the presence of an authentic, unpretentious person who loved God and shared his gifts with them.

We all can be modest people. It takes humility and self-effacing generosity. We move away from promoting ourselves and our accomplishments in order to use our God-given gifts which naturally help us serve others. He has given us all gifts to share. We move ourselves aside and allow God to speak and act through us. This is how we walk modestly in the world.

What can you do to demonstrate modesty to others?

BECOMING INFLUENTIAL

It is my prayer that your love may abound more and more,
with knowledge and all discernment, so that you may
approve what is excellent, and so be pure and blameless for
the day of Christ.

PHILIPPIANS 1:9-10 ESV

There are clear strategies used by people to infiltrate our
thinking and change our behavior. This is not a conspiracy
theory; it is a known method used on the public in
advertising, motivational talks, and even education. It has
been demonstrated that when you can get someone to sing
the tune, repeat the phrase, or believe in the motto, you can
influence how they shop, think, and behave.

The primary goal of advertising is to persuade customers to
acquire the product. But we see this also in music—secular
and Christian. Vision statements at work use this form
of manipulation. Schools and universities are targets for
politicians so they can change someone's thinking even
before people are old enough to vote or as they reach that
age. The proven path is to get them young, repeat what
they need to learn for the benefit of your special interest
group, and thereby influence society. It is why we need
knowledgeable and discriminating people to protect those
we serve until Christ returns.

How can you improve your knowledge of God?

EMOTIONAL STATE

Love one another with brotherly affection.
Outdo one another in showing honor.

ROMANS 12:10 ESV

We may think of honor as esteeming someone, but when Scripture says to give honor to one another, what does it look like in a practical way? This means that we demonstrate regard for others' needs before attending to our own. We do this not just practically, but also spiritually and emotionally.

In our daily interactions, it is pretty common to disregard emotions and just stick to the facts, but we need to practice paying attention to our internal cues in order to grow as disciples of Christ. Emotions drive our interactions with others, and when we are not observant of them, we are most likely to dishonor one another. Reactive emotions occur when we protect ourselves and lash out at others. As we mature, we become more attentive to our emotional states, and we learn to love those around us better. Awareness helps us maintain self-control, and from this place we can serve others which is a way we can show honor.

How can you honor those you work with today? How do you encourage people to be aware of their own emotional states?

MAY

Humble yourselves before the Lord,
and he will lift you up.

JAMES 4:10 NIV

PROVE YOURSELF

Prove yourselves to be blameless and innocent, children of God above reproach in the midst of a crooked and perverse generation, among whom you appear as lights in the world.

PHILIPPIANS 2:15 NASB

Have you ever been in an argument with someone, and they ask you to prove what you're saying? When this occurs, we often refer to our favorite sources and speak about the facts as we know them. It's harder with personal details in terms of who did what and such because that's based on what we remember, and memory is subjective.

Let's think about this today: we are constantly being challenged by the world to prove that we personally know and love God and that we belong to him. We have to show that we can live above reproach because of this connection. We know that his return is imminent, and we are surrounded by the perversion of what God has created. Money is king, sex is corrupt, relationships are transitory, and idol worship is honored as good. Worship of the one, true God is denigrated and ridiculed. The evidence of our faith is seen in the sacrifices we make every day as we follow him. It is also witnessed in the brotherhood of believers. We know that people will know the love of God when they see how we treat one another.

What about your actions to other believers gives testimony to your faith in Christ?

BEAUTY IN NATURE

How right they are to adore you.

SONG OF SOLOMON 1:4 NLT

When we get out in nature and experience the beauty that is all around us, we begin to marvel at the greatness of God. This introspection does require us to take a pause in order to perceive this awesome planet. If we are on a mission for something else, we will miss all that is good sitting right in front of us. There are countless days in daily living when we walk along the same roads or drive to the same places, yet we do not see the beauty that is evident along our journeys.

Today, pause to acknowledge and adore the God who made the stars, the moon, and the skies. Look at the earth and its beauty in the trees and the plants that abound upon it. Be inspired by the ocean with its tranquility and beautiful volatility. All of it calls out praises to the Creator as it magnifies his brilliance. How right it is to admire what he has made, and to glorify him for his creation. He created all this wonder—the universe, the plants, and the birds and animals—and at the center of it all is us, his personal favorite.

What can you praise him for today? What has captured your heart in his creation?

GROOMED

I praise you because you remember me in everything, and you follow closely the teachings just as I gave them to you.

1 CORINTHIANS 11:2 NCV

It is a gratifying feeling to groom someone for a role and see them fulfill it with excellence. It reflects well on us as leaders and teachers, but it is also satisfying to have someone that believes in what was taught and embraces it successfully.

Would it be much different for God? He has emotions just as we do. He enjoys seeing us take on his Spirit and act as Jesus would. His purpose in sending the Holy Spirit was to help us by providing a teacher, guide, and counselor. If we learn to tap into the significant gift that his Spirit is to us, what could happen? What limit is there on people who are tutored by the Holy Spirit?

Think about people you have mentored. What makes you proud of them, and do you think God looks at you in a similar way?

Speaking Up

My eager expectation and hope is that I will not be
ashamed about anything, but that now as always, with all
courage, Christ will be highly honored in my body, whether
by life or by death.

PHILIPPIANS 1:20 CSB

Speaking up takes a level of bravery. Within any group
of people, perhaps even in a team which we are currently
leading, there are a few people who will share a thought or
insight effortlessly; there are others who struggle to speak
up in any situation. The silent ones do not necessarily lack
an opinion; they just have something stronger driving them
to stay quiet.

We have to specifically invite the less bold to speak, and
then we also sometimes have to quiet down the bold. And
when we do either, we do not want members of our group
to feel shame. Rather, our hope is that each person will gain
confidence in their abilities to express their thoughts and
articulate them with clear reasoning.

*What do you do well to help balance opinions with those
you lead?*

STRONG COMMUNITY

"Where two or three gather together as my followers,
I am there among them."

MATTHEW 18:20 NLT

We receive a sense of belonging when a group of individuals accepts us as a part of them. Community is an important part of being human, and for those that don't have a community of their own, their lives can be lonely. We see more and more stories these days where loneliness can end in tragedy. We all need to belong. Our work communities have lately gained value as people give credibility to these relationships as more than just a place to accomplish a job.

Friendships and a sense of comradery have increased in the workplace. Part of this evolution has occurred as the percent of women in the workforce has doubled since the 1920s and there is now a balance between the genders. When social communities are healthier, our work communities develop stronger connections. Within these improved groups we have the opportunity to invite believers to engage together in fellowship. Hopefully through this we can share the love of Christ with those who lack a sense of community outside of work.

What community of believers are you connected to and how deep are those connections?

FRIENDLY FORTITUDE

Accept each other just as Christ has accepted you so that
God will be given glory.

ROMANS 15:7 NLT

Our demeanor as Christians should be loving. God is love
and we are his ambassadors. We do not want to reflect
judgment, harshness, or hatred. We want to maintain an
approachable persona. This is not easy in a world that so
grossly maligns our faith, nor is it easy to refrain from
worldly thinking when we are too open to the messages
around us that do not glorify God. Friendship with the
world is enmity toward God. So how do we maintain
a gracious, outgoing, and responsive posture without
welcoming in the same sins that beset those who are not
pursuing Christ? The answer is within us since the Holy
Spirit indwells us.

We can stand for righteousness while we are still welcoming
to those who are seeking Christ. We do not have to accept
sin to accept the person who yet lives in their sinful nature.
Rejecting someone for their sin is the world's teaching.
Christ accepted those who repented and was clear that
they should therefore go and live without sin. He didn't
say, "Sin all you want, and I will love and accept you." Our
friendliness toward the world is to be tempered with God's
truth and righteousness.

*Does your friendliness with the world differentiate you, or
does it make you one of them?*

ROADBLOCKS

Though we walk in the flesh, we are not waging war according to the flesh. For the weapons of our warfare are not of the flesh but have divine power to destroy strongholds.

2 CORINTHIANS 10:3-4 ESV

It is easy for us to get locked into perceiving people as our adversaries. After all, they are tangible representations of their own sin, as are we. Satan and his demons are not so easily identified. However, they are very active and are constantly looking for opportunities to inflame relationships.

As we mature in our faith, we become wiser in how we approach troubling situations. First, we know the enemy is at work, so we are alert. Second, we have learned the power of prayer and when and how to hunker down in the Spirit. We learn with maturity how to rest in God and allow him to fight our battles. When we pray, God moves on our behalf, and we learn to align our actions with his intentions. This is especially effective when you face human roadblocks. Sometimes it appears a person is opposing you, but really it is the enemy using them as a barrier to God's work. God has the power to break those spiritual walls down and to help you be the one who overcomes.

Can you recall times when you surrendered a situation to God in prayer and he moved on your behalf?

OPERATING IN GRACE

By grace you have been saved through faith,
and that not of yourselves; it is the gift of God.

EPHESIANS 2:8 NKJV

Graceful: it simply means full of grace. Gracious: this is more like unmerited favor or receiving something you don't deserve. We have been given grace by God through the death and resurrection of Christ, and that is the forgiveness of our sins. Do we pause to mull on this and truly allow it to sink in? His grace was not just a onetime act; it keeps flowing for us. Every day. Every sin. Because of our sinful nature, we act in an unholy manner before a holy God. Every time we sin, we look to Jesus and repent. By his sacrifice, God forgives us. He wipes away our sins. We don't deserve it, and we shouldn't receive such grace, but we do.

We are challenged to replicate this grace with one another, especially in our roles as overseers and leaders. How do we purposefully exemplify the Spirit of Christ in us each day? We do this by showing others the same grace that he has shown us.

Ask the Holy Spirit to speak to you. Are there any areas where grace is not operating in your life?

DAILY DECISIONS

"Love your enemies! Do good to them. Lend to them without expecting to be repaid. Then your reward from heaven will be very great, and you will truly be acting as children of the Most High, for he is kind to those who are unthankful and wicked."

LUKE 6:35 NLT

Doing good to those who have hurt you is a tough ask. In fact, it is downright impossible apart from the goodness of God moving through the believer's heart. If you have ever been crossed by a business associate or someone you are working with at church, it can make you angry and hurt enough to want to sever any future relationship. The last thing you want to do is show any goodness toward them. And you certainly don't want to lend anything to them as today's verse says to do.

But we recognize our position in this life as temporary, and we have a great inheritance in Christ. This allows us to bless others, even our enemies. We can hold loosely to things of this earth and, consequently, hold firmly to the hope of the age to come. We look forward to a much greater time of wealth and prosperity for us in the everlasting life to come.

How does eternity weigh into your daily decisions?

BALANCED FEAR

"Fear not, for I am with you;
be not dismayed, for I am your God;
I will strengthen you, I will help you,
I will uphold you with my righteous right hand."

ISAIAH 41:10 ESV

Some fear is healthy. Too much can disable a person, but the right amount can be life giving. There are few truly fearless people because those who are tend to take things far enough that they either learn to fear or they are no longer alive. Fear helps us to restrain our actions and words. When we demonstrate courage, strength, and bravery, we overcome fear by choice. We look it in the eye and tell it, *not this time, my friend. I have bold things to do.*

God gives us the ability and the confidence to be fearless in the face of opposition. He often tells us in Scripture that he is with us. We don't need to be afraid; we can be courageous. In him lies the strength to step up in a situation. When we fall, he is there to catch us. He either restores us in his love or receives us into eternity. Either way, we are safe in him.

As you have grown in your leadership, how has God helped you overcome fear?

SHARP FOCUS

"The one who endures to the end will be saved."

MATTHEW 24:13 NLT

One of the qualities of successful business owners is focus. It is a gift to be tenacious when it comes to reaching a goal and not letting go until it is completed. When things get tough, they get tougher. When it is time to throw in the towel, they go down with the ship. Endurance in a successful relationship sometimes requires at least one person to acquire the tenacity of a bulldog in order to never, ever give up. Focus is also found in the athlete who comes home with the championship trophy. They have such a deep concentration that are not distracted by less important goals, and they can even compete through pain in order to achieve the win.

Jesus had this kind of focus throughout his life. He wouldn't let go of his goal even when Satan tried to tempt him with so-called shortcuts. He suffered immensely to the point of shedding his blood on that cruel cross, but he never wavered in his commitment to finish what he started. This is the kind of focus that inspires.

How can you sharpen your focus?

REST IN ACTIVITY

"My presence will go with you,
and I will give you rest."

EXODUS 33:14 ESV

What does it mean for you to rest? Most of us think about
the different ways we relax or how we take a break from our
labors. But how often do we tie rest to the importance of
taking time to wait on God? Do we consider that if we issue
an invitation to God to be involved in what we are doing
will give us the rest we need? When he speaks about being
present with us and going with us into whatever we are
doing, he is not talking about being inactive. He is talking
about our need to appeal to him and for him to join in in
what we are doing.

Resting in God is about going through our days while
trusting him to be with us in all we do. It is a difficult task
to be so attentive to God because we are inherently self-
reliant. He challenges us to learn how to invite him to be
a part of our everyday lives. When we do, he gives us the
peace we need. What makes our days hard? Anxiety and
worry do. God promises that when he is with us, we can
rest because we will have his peace.

*What can you do today to allow his peace to give you rest
while staying busy at work?*

TITLES

Him we proclaim, warning everyone and teaching everyone
with all wisdom, that we may present everyone mature in
Christ. For this I toil, struggling with all his energy that he
powerfully works within me.

COLOSSIANS 1:28-29 ESV

We work hard. This is how we were able to get to where
we are now in life. There is no denying that diligence,
endurance, labor, and intentionality all help us to achieve
success. We also know that God has worked in us and has
placed us where we are today.

Without his help, guidance, and leadership we would not
be where we are. It is his energy working powerfully within
us that drives us in the right direction. We recognize our
dependence upon him, and we pray for him to continue
his work in us with grace and patience. We desire him to
help us present leadership qualities that reflect him. We are
willing to be stretched by him so that he may be glorified
through us for the benefit of others. In God's economy,
leadership and sacrifice go hand-in-hand. We admit that
the title we hold is about him and not about us.

*How can you use your title to glorify God and help others to
mature in Christ?*

UNIVERSAL SOLUTION

Blessed is the one who perseveres under trial because, having stood the test, that person will receive the crown of life that the Lord has promised to those who love him.

JAMES 1:12 NIV

Every adult on the planet has faced adversity at some stage in their life. Most of us can tell a story about how we overcame it. Is it possible for us to all work together in order to figure out a formula that would give the best way to beat life's troubles? It is unlikely that any formulae would become a universal solution.

We are each so different and the conditions we face are so varied. However, there is a secret that not all people know, and it can be universally applied to every problem. It allows us to endure unbelievable adversity. The potential of it is found in every person, but it is not present until it is properly activated. It is a simple word: hope. But it is not a common hope such as the world talks about it. It is a special hope; it is the hope that is placed in Jesus Christ and our resurrection to eternal life.

When you go through difficulties, how do you sense God's strength, and what do you hope in?

FOLLOW ME

The generous man will be prosperous,
And one who gives others plenty of water
will himself be given plenty.

PROVERBS 11:25 NASB

The altruistic bachelor grew up in a simple countryside town. He was independently successful and quite the catch for any woman. However, his true passion was to care for his family and those he was responsible for. He spent his days traveling and helping people. He handed out pearls of wisdom to those who were willing to hear. People marveled at his giving heart because he selflessly shared his time, resources, and talent with anyone who needed him. When he left a city, the place was abuzz with talk about his actions. The crazy thing was that he never asked for anything in return except for genuine relationships. His words were a simple call: follow me.

Jesus, the truly benevolent man, discipled with care, kindness, compassion, and sacrifice. He didn't need what others had because the Father took care of him.

In what ways does God demonstrate generosity through you toward those whom you lead?

WE CAN LAUGH

We laughed and laughed and overflowed with gladness.
We were left shouting for joy and singing your praise.

PSALM 126:2 TPT

Have you ever wondered if God has fun? Why do you think
he made laughter? We are made in our Creator's image,
so he laughs too! God is not so modest or serious that
he cannot laugh. In fact, look at the rest of his creation.
Perhaps he made some things simply so we can laugh.

Have you ever seen a gobi jerboa or a proboscis monkey?
Look up images of them and see what you think. There are
so many different, funny things that God created. When we
begin to realize that God wants us to be joyful because he
is joyful, we start to understand him more. Yes, he wants
us to be holy, too, but the two are not mutually exclusive.
He is both joyful and holy. God delights when we gather
with those people we work and church with and can laugh,
enjoying each other and reflecting on his goodness and love.

How does the Holy Spirit help you to lighten up and laugh?
Do you think he is only somber?

A CERTAIN ABILITY

I can do everything through Christ,
who gives me strength.

PHILIPPIANS 4:13 NLT

God has given each one of us certain abilities. Whether
these gifts are great or small in our own eyes, God intends
them to be used significantly for the kingdom. When we
read a Scripture verse like the one above, or when Paul
wrote that God's strength is made perfect in his own
weakness, we may feel that we cannot really rely on any
of our own capabilities to accomplish much of anything.
Perhaps God would be displeased that we are not relying on
him more?

This misunderstanding of the purpose of our characteristics
is not of God. He wants us to use our talents for him. In
fact, he uniquely made us and created in us these traits
to use for him. If we refrain or withhold ourselves in any
way, we end up promoting ourselves and not growing the
kingdom. We are naturally and uniquely us, so we will
be displaying and engaging with these abilities without
awareness or effort on our own part. We can, however,
choose to use them for God and deny the use of them when
they only pump up ourselves if we are aware. We should
hone all of our skills in the workplace. We each have a
unique role which allows us to encourage gifts in ourselves
and others and to use them for God's kingdom.

How can you encourage your team to use their gifts for God?

EXTENDING KINDNESS

Be kind to one another, tenderhearted,
forgiving one another, as God in Christ forgave you.

 EPHESIANS 4:32 ESV

Kindness shows up within humanity in many ways as simple compassion or consideration for those we encounter along the way. It's the attitude of helping others and improving their circumstances through our thoughtful, charitable deeds. We are encouraged in this verse to not only show kindness, but to also couple it with forgiveness. To bless those who have hurt us with not only forgiveness but also with tenderness.

Of course, Paul is writing to the church in order to teach those who believe how to how we should treat our brothers and sisters, but if we extend this mercy to those outside the church what impact would that have? How different would the world's perception of Christians be if we were all as kind as Christ was? What would it look like if this were happening today within the members of the teams you lead?

Outside of your immediate circle, how do you care for those in need?

GOOD INFLUENCE

Do not be deceived: "Bad company ruins good morals."

1 CORINTHIANS 15:33 ESV

The leader never knew how he was affecting the others. He just hung out with the group and spent time with people. It wasn't like he was intentionally trying to sway anyone or encourage them specifically. He just liked being with them and they seemed to enjoy being with him as well. They would go on hikes, worship God, and hang out over coffee as they waxed philosophical. He wasn't the leader of the group. But to several of them, he was that guy. They looked up to him. They saw someone they wanted to be like, and he liked the same things they did. They saw a man who loved and worshiped God, and he was entirely a really good person.

It can be surprising to us when we are seen as influencers in other people's lives. So much about being in this position is about the perception others hold about this person. Having a leadership title makes the position obvious, but that doesn't necessarily mean that they fulfill the most valued qualities in other people's eyes. There are many with a title who have little influence.

As people follow your example, how are they influenced to behave toward others?

IMPORTANT ALIGNMENT

We are his workmanship, created in Christ Jesus for good
works, which God prepared beforehand, that we should
walk in them.

EPHESIANS 2:10 ESV

What do we devote our time, money, and talents to? Those
choices are a good measure of what we consider important.
What we consider important may actually be different
than how we live. This is where we find the most revealing
contradictions in our lives. Do the things we consider
important align with the things we spend our time, money,
and talents on? If so, we are principled and live honestly in
accordance with ourselves. If the things we value are not
aligned with how we live, our lives will feel conflicted. We
will have unsettled hearts and will likely be unhappy.

We find alignment between our deeds and our souls when
we seek God. He helps us find the vital pursuits which we
should be doing that line us up with our honest God-given
passions and interests. Continue to pour out your heart to
God and ask him to help align what is important to you
with what you are actively doing day-to-day. In this very
moment, you are on the right track.

*What do you want to do with your life that you have you not
done yet?*

CORE NEEDS

We are afflicted in every way, but not crushed; perplexed,
but not driven to despair; persecuted, but not forsaken;
struck down, but not destroyed; always carrying in the
body the death of Jesus, so that the life of Jesus may also be
manifested in our bodies.

2 CORINTHIANS 4:8-9 ESV

For many in the world, affliction and adversity look
vastly different than what we face in our modernized
society. Some people fear the complete destruction of
their homelands. Others are downtrodden as they try to
survive the next few weeks without crops or shelter for their
families. Despite the differences between countries, we all
face troubles in our souls. We all, perhaps surprisingly, are
challenged by feelings of abandonment, shame, and guilt.
These afflict all mankind equally. We all face the core needs
of our hearts by way of the inner struggles of humanity.

Whatever our lot in life may be and regardless of how
adversity presents itself, we have within us the hope of
resurrection. We shall not succumb to a point where
circumstances or shame cause us to be abandoned because
we are redeemed. Christ died for us and has chosen to make
us his forever. We want to share this good news with others.

*When you're going through your own troubles, how can you
pause and draw from outside yourself in order to place your
hope in the resurrection?*

SUCCESSFUL SEASON

> He saved us, not because of works done by us in righteousness, but according to his own mercy, by the washing of regeneration and renewal of the Holy Spirit.

TITUS 3:5 ESV

A satisfying part of each day is being able to look back at any accomplishments, at least on those days when we have been productive. There is a known release of endorphins when we complete tasks, so it's easy to know why it feels good. When these accomplishments mount up and we have a successful season, we start to feel pretty good about ourselves. The danger is that we can become self-reliant and therefore dismiss our need to connect with God.

It is wisdom to remember that most of us have experienced enough tribulations in life to know that we must suppress this sin and be on our knees before our merciful Savior. We acknowledge the strength and urging of the Holy Spirit who renews us daily. Jesus is the one who saves us, and no amount of successes on our part will liberate us from the guilt of sin and our deserved death. This brings us back down to earth and reminds us of the great one who saves and is worthy of our honor.

What are you thankful for today?

PAUSE AND REMEMBER

"Peace I leave with you, My peace I give to you; not as the world gives do I give to you. Let not your heart be troubled, neither let it be afraid."

JOHN 14:27 NKJV

Take a moment to think about your favorite place to visit or live when you were growing up. Why is it a favorite? What do you feel when you think about it? Most often those special places give us a sense of peace. They conjure up feelings of rest, relaxation, fun, and special times with friends and family. When you think about your favorite place, can you imagine God visiting you there? Perhaps you can envision him walking with you as your family and friends used to do.

God is smiling at you and pleased to be with you. In your heart, there is a sense of inexpressible joy and pleasure. God knows you and understands your questions and your troubles. Set all of those questions and troubles aside. Pause and remember your favorite place. Invite God into those feelings and allow his peace to embrace you. He can calm your fears and anxieties.

What does God say to you when you're pondering your favorite place?

A Mature Team

Until we all attain to the unity of the faith and of the
knowledge of the Son of God, to mature manhood, to the
measure of the stature of the fullness of Christ.

EPHESIANS 4:13 ESV

Mature teams have character which has been built out of a
strong sense of shared purpose. That foundation has carried
the members through various trials and unified them in a
way that can only be accomplished by forging those trials
together. The first example that comes to mind is a tight-
knit military team whose members have trained together
for months and struggled together through adversity.
Each member supports the others so when one is weak,
the strength of the group carries them. When they face
a difficulty or threat, they naturally unite against it with
the force of the whole group. What makes such a team
unique is the hardships they have shared. Their lives have
formed this particular group character, and the team has a
consequentially developed maturity because of it.

This is what we are encouraged to seek as believers. We
need to exist as a team of people who have matured
through adversity and are now able to do what God
requires regardless of what hardships may be ahead.

*Can you identify the challenges your team has overcome and
encourage them for it?*

THE GREATEST HOPE

> Since we are his true children, we qualify to share all his
> treasures, for indeed, we are heirs of God himself. And
> since we are joined to Christ, we also inherit all that he is
> and all that he has. We will experience being co-glorified
> with him provided that we accept his sufferings as our own.
>
> ROMANS 8:17 TPT

Is there a human on the planet who has not suffered? No,
we all suffer in some form every day. That reality could
tend to depress us. We are stuck in a sinful world where evil
surrounds us and people die every day. In fact, sociologists
state that studies show our spirits are dampened and our
culture is depressed. We are inundated by media and
information, we have too many possessions, and there's
pervasive cultural conflict. What can change? Who has any
hope of anything different?

We do! The people of God know joy and peace in their
lives. We are transformed and set free from sin and death.
We look forward to the greatest hope for all mankind which
is resurrection to everlasting life on a renewed earth with
Jesus as our King.

How can you share your hope with others today?

HONORABLE

If anyone cleanses himself from what is dishonorable, he will be a vessel for honorable use, set apart as holy, useful to the master of the house, ready for every good work.

2 TIMOTHY 2:21 ESV

Who doesn't want to win? We want to be the person that gets top honors! "You didn't win, but hey, look on the bright side. You got an honorable mention." Who wants that? What if the prize itself was being honorable and had nothing to do with winning. That is our goal as believers and especially as leaders—that we are seen as upright and worthy.

Even in defeat, honorable people are respected. They are humble enough to concede when they don't win. They demonstrate decency and worthiness by competing well but not always having to be top dog. The just and humble people focus on honoring and serving others, loving them well, and doing what is right. The honorable ones are principled and respectable people whom we admire, not because they win but because of their character whether they win or not.

What in your life is admirable and brings honor to others?

POSITION IN LIFE

Christ suffered for our sins once for all time.
He never sinned, but he died for sinners to bring you
safely home to God. He suffered physical death,
but he was raised to life in the Spirit.

1 PETER 3:18 NLT

As competent people who have relied a great deal on
ourselves to get things accomplished, it can be difficult to
allow others to help. Usually we find that it is just easier
to get tasks done ourselves. Why take the time and effort
to explain the details of a job to others when they could
possibly mess it up anyway? This independent spirit can
also mess with our faith. Do we really need a Savior, or can
we be good enough on our own? We do not sin like other
people; we are pretty good, really. Ha! God laughs at us.

We are so simple-minded about our position in life. He
looks at our independence as resistance to him—as sin.
He sees our successes as a failure to depend upon him. Yet
when we come to him in repentance, he is so gentle and
kind. He is gracious and merciful, and he welcomes us with
a warm embrace and a smiling face. He is a good Father.

If God asked you what you think of him what would you say?

PRECIOUS LIFE

> "The thief comes only to steal and kill and destroy.
> I came that they may have life and have it abundantly."
>
> JOHN 10:10 ESV

Life is such a beautiful thing. From birth until death, life is precious. Every person has great value and purpose for their existence. Each one is meaningful. Life is precious and valuable to God. Living is a different beast. Living is hard. We navigate through it with chaos on one side and order on the other. Pain, sorrow, joy, and pleasure are all mixed together in daily living. Living is troublesome for most of us because in one minute we are in a place of bliss and then— wham! We are taken into the dark hole of loss and sadness. All it takes is for a precious life to be lost.

In the middle of it all is our God. He is the rock. He is the giver and taker of life; he's the living and active redeemer. He changes everything because though living may be troublesome, in him we have everlasting satisfaction. Not only does he provide a secure future, but he also gives us happiness in the midst of troubles.

How does God give you joy even in the difficulties of life?

ENGAGEMENT LEVEL

Since God loved us that much,
we surely ought to love each other.

1 JOHN 4:11 NLT

Have you ever owned a dog? If you got it shortly after it was weaned, you will probably remember your little puppy with his tail flopping around. They are the most lovable little creatures. It's heartwarming to watch that little ball of fur trying to walk or run around as he plays and nips, rolls and yips. Then when they are exhausted, they curl up and fall asleep on you. There has to be touch; they need to be next to you. It makes them all the more lovable.

There is something about certain people that just makes them lovable. Science would say that they exude oxytocin: a hormone that increases positive attitude and bonding with others. It is a connection hormone that increases trust. It is the lovable hormone. We all have it, not just the hormone but also the ability to love and be lovable. We can increase it, too, with simple practices around eye contact, touch, active listening, and reading non-verbal cues, all which create connectivity between humans.

What can you do to increase your engagement levels with others and increase healthy connections?

CONNECTED BY PRAYER

Pray in the Spirit at all times and on every occasion.
Stay alert and be persistent in your prayers for
all believers everywhere.

EPHESIANS 6:18 NLT

Can you imagine in the midst of a team meeting you
suddenly start to pray out loud? People would likely be
shocked. What on earth was that about? What does it look
like for us to be praying in the Spirit constantly? Most often
we pray silently and internally since prayer has to do with
aligning our hearts with God's Spirit. When we live our
lives in constant prayer, we remain alert and more easily
sense the movements of God.

Jesus walked this way when he was on the earth. He said
that everything he did was what the Father was doing. In
other words, he was so consistently connected to the Father
through the Spirit that he instinctively did what the Father
wanted him to do. How great for us! We have been given
the same opportunity and as we practice this level of prayer,
we will become perfected in it.

*What can you do to make decisions prayerfully throughout
the day?*

In Spite of Failure

By the grace given to me I say to everyone among you not
to think of himself more highly than he ought to think,
but to think with sober judgment, each according to the
measure of faith that God has assigned.

ROMANS 12:3 ESV

The old man looked in the mirror and considered the
wrinkles under his stubble and the thinning hair that was
slowly turning gray. Lately he had even started to look a bit
scraggly. His eyes were still bright, and his heart was full of
love, but his body was wearing out. What had he done with
his life? What great things had he accomplished? He was no
saint, that was certain. Many of those wrinkles felt like deep
reminders of his failures. The shrinking hairline caused
him to think about the past and the times he had failed
in his relationships. Yet, that was the beauty of taking this
moment to ponder and reflect.

Despite all the weighty thoughts, there was great life in the
old man. His heart was full because his faith in God had
motivated him to revisit those broken relationships and to
reconcile with others when he could. His deep love for others
above his own selfishness was entirely because of his Savior.

When you reflect upon your character, in spite of any
failures, what are the great things God has done?

JUNE

Commit your way to the LORD;
trust in him and he will do this:
He will make your righteous reward
shine like the dawn,
your vindication like the noonday sun.

PSALM 37:5-6 NIV

CLOUDINESS AND FOG

"You also must be ready, for the Son of Man
is coming at an hour you do not expect."

MATTHEW 24:44 ESV

If there is cloudiness in the mind of a leader, there is
fog in the minds of those who follow them. Therefore,
one of the greatest assets a leader can offer is good, clear
communication which of course falls out of good, clear
thinking. We know that when we are indecisive, others will
be unsure, unsettled, and ultimately unproductive. Firm
decisions and a straightforward way of communicating with
them are what help others know their roles and understand
what is expected of them while they fulfill those roles.

Jesus was clear about what to expect in the end times and
he gave a great amount of detail about the surrounding
events in this hour. Should those alive when the end times
happen be surprised? Not if they are ready and have been
attentive to the signs. Not if they are reading the Word
and listening to the Holy Spirit speak to them as the signs
increase and the moment approaches. Our leader made
things clear—he aligned our roles with his goals, and we
can be ready as we stay attuned to his plan.

*The Holy Spirit speaks when he is preparing his followers.
What has he been saying to you?*

THE SAME

Jesus Christ is the same
yesterday and today and forever.

HEBREWS 13:8 ESV

There is a photo of a man standing in the entrance to a lighthouse. Behind him a giant wave crashes around and over the tower; water sprays out as the surge collapses around him. He remains steadfast. Not even the mighty wave moves him. He looks toward the lens at the photographer with a marked peacefulness, knowing he is secure. It is an intriguing photo.

Contrasts in life bring distinction: bright stars against the black night, icebergs on the dark seas, blue skies over desert landscapes, and dry winter trees amongst new spring shoots. So many things in nature show variation and change. Our lives twist and turn, undulating between chaos and order. Somewhere in the middle, holding it all together, is our mighty God. He stands still. He is constant and unbroken by change. He remains stable in the storm like the man in the photo. His position is eternal, and he remains constant.

Because God is consistent, how does this help you through the difficulty that faces every overseer?

Discovering Life

"I am the resurrection and the life. Whoever believes in me, though he die, yet shall he live, and everyone who lives and believes in me shall never die. Do you believe this?"

JOHN 11:25-26 ESV

Jesus made it clear that death comes to all, but eternal death only comes to those who don't choose eternal life. What seems clear to us is vague to the rest of the world. Jesus is the resurrection, the eternal life we are looking for. Even though believers know this truth, there is a hope amongst those who reject God that man can somehow find a way to live longer or even forever.

Will science somehow make the immense breakthrough that would be required to forever change life and death? No. It is a futile pursuit. Do those people think about the repercussions of living forever? What would man's resolution for global overpopulation be like? We shudder to think about it. The Bible is clear that each person has an end, but because of the resurrection of Christ, we can have everlasting life with him. Jesus is the discovery that science seems to be looking for. He is the true source of life. We believe in his truth, which shows us the way to infinity and beyond.

Do you believe that the only way to live forever is though the resurrection of the Christ?

ETERNAL PROMISES

"Don't store up treasures here on earth, where moths eat them and rust destroys them, and where thieves break in and steal. Store your treasures in heaven, where moths and rust cannot destroy, and thieves do not break in and steal."

MATTHEW 6:19-20 NLT

Security has many dimensions; spiritual, emotional, personal, corporate, and financial. But how certain is it? Can all of it be stripped away in an instant? In this life, where moths, rust, thieves, and harmful people seem to dominate, our protection and surety is found in our eternal promises.

When we consider what we have, whatever kind of possession it may be, we should ask the question if we can take it into eternity. As we ask this, it should give us a measure of how valuable it can be to us. Then perhaps we may ask, can this help others into eternity, again arming us with the same measure. Ultimately, we will be left with little to value but our person, and the relationships we have with others. It is why Jesus invested in people. He used his time, talent, and treasure for eternity alone.

How can you encourage those you shepherd to trust all they have to Jesus?

MOOT POINT

It is not that we think we are qualified to do anything on our own. Our qualification comes from God.

2 CORINTHIANS 3:5 NLT

Why are you interested in the job of leadership? What qualifications or experiences do you have? You have had these questions before, and you may have even asked them recently. When you ask someone about their qualifications, what do you really want to hear? Do you want a list, or do you want to know how the interviewee can competently and skillfully complete the tasks related to the roles and responsibilities of the job.

Paul wrote to the church in Corinth that his qualifications did not come from himself but from God. It's kind of a moot point because it was evident in Paul that the power and anointing of the Holy Spirit was active throughout his work. The activity of the Holy Spirit is also evident in those of us today who are leading people because of a faith-based calling. We know we are qualified to minister, not because of who we are, but because God is doing the work through us. It is his power at work in us and this is the source of our confidence.

As a conduit for the Holy Spirit, what can you do to improve his flow of spiritual strength through your life?

A Humble Man

"I have given you an example,
that you also should do just as I have done to you."

JOHN 13:15 ESV

The businessman was the kind of person who was easy to get to know. He was tall, had a slight build, and exuded his friendly warmth in a great smile. He had a solid job in a global company and managed teams all over the world. People wouldn't know if he was a simple clerk or a powerful leader because he was a humble man. He never promoted himself but instead demonstrated goodness to his family, his church, his work, and even people he met in passing. He was always well thought of amongst his peers. He was a truly respectable man.

The test came when his youngest child was diagnosed with leukemia while still a boy. The businessman paused everything else so his home life could adjust. Even so, not much truly changed because he took the challenges in stride. He helped his wife and his children through physical and emotional difficulties, and gracefully accepted help from those who offered. Through it all he continued to encourage everyone and to smile. Once his young son was through the worst of it, he had more gray hair, but his character hadn't shifted. He was anchored in Christ.

What would people consider and observe as respectable in you?

INTONATION

"You shall follow the LORD your God and fear Him; and
you shall keep His commandments, listen to His voice,
serve Him, and cling to Him."

DEUTERONOMY 13:4 NASB

The first thing we notice when we raise children is that
babies know the sound of their parents' voices at birth. They
may even have happy movements while still in utero when
they hear mom and dad speaking or singing. As children
start to adjust to the world around them, they witness our
responses to various experiences. They start to react to the
intonations of our voices and learn what to expect when we
speak with a soothing sound or issue a sharp warning. It's
not necessarily the words we speak but the tone we use. As
they grow, they become attentive to how we say things as
well as what we say.

In a similar manner, we must learn to listen to God's Spirit.
Even new believers may pick up on the intonations of God's
voice when he is making it clear that something is good and
something else is not. But as we mature, we do learn also
how to distinguish the variances in the voice of the Lord. As
this occurs, we can listen to him and reverently follow his
leadership.

*How can you develop a deeper sensitivity to the Holy Spirit
and cling to God's Word?*

SYMPATHETIC SACRIFICE

All of you, be like-minded, be sympathetic,
love one another, be compassionate and humble.

1 PETER 3:8 NIV

It takes a leader with good character to show authentic
sympathy. Jesus came to earth so he could sympathize with
us in our human, weak condition. He didn't stand back.
He fully threw himself into our mess. His compassion
and kindness were demonstrated in his sacrifice, and that
is important to note. Sympathy does not occur without a
willingness to take the focus off us and to allow the time
to consider what others are experiencing. When we have
properly thought about others, we can act with kindness,
love, and humility. And that humility means that we place
others before ourselves.

Jesus could have stayed with his Father. He chose to come
to us and experience a human life while still being God.
He faced our temptations, anxieties, and emotions. He felt
our joy and pleasure. His authentic kindness caused him to
come as a man so we would know that he fully understands
what we experience.

*If you thought Jesus was praying for you at this moment,
what would you ask him to pray for?*

METAMORPHOSIS

Flesh and blood cannot inherit the kingdom of God, nor
does the perishable inherit the imperishable. Behold! I tell
you a mystery. We shall not all sleep, but we shall all be
changed, in a moment, in the twinkling of an eye,
at the last trumpet.

1 CORINTHIANS 15:50-52 ESV

Sin is ugly. There is no way to paint it to make it pretty. And
to a holy God, sin is abhorrent. He detests it, and never
wants any of us to revel in it. Sin is so foreign to the nature
of God that flesh and blood as we know it now will not
be accepted into God's kingdom. Because of sin, God will
destroy what is now and make it new. What a miracle that
he speaks life into existence!

Consider the caterpillar which analogizes the changes we
will experience when we enter the kingdom of God. We
are slow, grounded, spiky creatures in our human, sinful
form, and we will be transformed into beautiful, fluttering
creatures which bring joy to the Almighty One. Jesus is the
patient farmer anticipating the release of his kaleidoscope
of butterflies. Consider, however, that as forgiven
caterpillars right now, we are fat with happiness and
gratitude for our coming redemption and transformation.

*How do God's promises of our future in eternity affect how
you lead others today?*

ALL THE MONEY

Tell them to use their money to do good. They should be
rich in good works and generous to those in need, always
being ready to share with others.

1 TIMOTHY 6:18 NLT

Having all the money in the world does not buy happiness.
Studies have shown that having a certain amount of wealth
does make people happier, but rather, it is dependent on a
person's spending habits. More possessions make for more
responsibilities and more worries, so people are not as
happy. More experiences, however, bring intermittent joy,
which is beneficial. Helping people is the most gratifying
way to use wealth, and God consistently reminds us that not
all treasures are currency. He gave us skills and experiences
which are valuable to the people who need them.

God has placed you in your current position so you can use
your specific gifts for others to be blessed. His goal is to use
you to be rich in good works for him! Remember that God
is your provider and all you need to serve others is given
specifically to you by him.

*How does your balance sheet of skills, resources, and
experiences affect your day-to-day perspective?*

THE SUFFERING ASPECT

The God of all grace, who called you to his eternal glory
in Christ, after you have suffered a little while, will himself
restore you and make you strong, firm and steadfast.

1 PETER 5:10 NIV

It seems that the suffering aspect of life is unavoidable. No
one really wants to embrace suffering, but some people
focus on it so much it seems that it is their lot. There is
no need to make suffering a focus. God has given us great
promises in him, including joy in this life. His Spirit is
given to us so that we may have joy, comfort, peace, and
pleasure despite the suffering.

Humans suffer; no one denies this. We know that Jesus and
every one of the disciples suffered immensely, they did not
succumb to it. Their strength and purpose can be seen in
how they overcame through the steadfast work of the Holy
Spirit. You have that same Spirit in you. Be encouraged to
call others into this same hope which you have, knowing
that this life is brief and our inheritance in an eternity with
our Savior is secure.

Despite what you experience with trials and tribulations,
how can your hope in Christ be a strength to you and a
witness to others?

GOD'S ART

We now have this light shining in our hearts, but we
ourselves are like fragile clay jars containing this great
treasure. This makes it clear that our great power is from
God, not from ourselves.

2 CORINTHIANS 4:7 NLT

This is an inspiring picture of us as believers. If we think
about clay jars, some would have cracks in them and
some would have holes through which a person could see
daylight. The jars are fragile enough that they can easily
chip, yet strong enough to hold water or wine for months at
a time. The jars are so beautiful that they even retain their
beauty when they are broken.

We are God's art. He draws us to himself, and we are
beautiful. And we desire to be those broken, beautiful
vessels that God uses to entice people to him. He is
powerful, and what he has accomplished in us is uniquely
wonderful. It is a worthy pursuit to know the Maker. We
may feel immense pressure to carry God's presence in a
way that glorifies him and is the right kind of attraction to
others for him. Thankfully, it is his Spirit in us that does this
work and we only have to be willing vessels to allow him to
shine through us.

*What treasure has God placed in you for others to see and to
glorify himself?*

NOT JUST OPTIMISM

Rejoice in hope, be patient in tribulation,
be constant in prayer.

ROMANS 12:12 ESV

As people of faith, we are to be optimistic about our futures. We have a hope that is undeniable, whether it is front and center in our lives or it is simply hovering in the recesses of our minds. Our hope is everlasting, and we know it to be true. We are clear on this: Christ is returning, and he will destroy Satan and his followers. He will restore the earth and we will dwell upon it with him for all eternity. That is not a naïve sentiment; it is firmly founded upon the testimonies of the witnesses to the death and resurrection of Christ and his ascension to the Father.

We have an incredible opportunity to share with others what is locked deeply within us. We possess liberty from sin, a resurrected body after death, and the Spirit of God living within us to affirm that we will receive these promises. We rejoice in this even in our difficult times because we know our God is a person of integrity who is truth and righteousness.

What is the most exciting aspect of your future in Christ?

TREMENDOUS

I saw one like a son of man, clothed in a robe reaching to the feet, and wrapped around the chest with a golden sash. His head and His hair were white like white wool, like snow; and His eyes were like a flame of fire. His feet were like burnished bronze when it has been heated to a glow in a furnace, and His voice was like the sound of many waters. In His right hand He held seven stars, and out of His mouth came a sharp two-edged sword; and His face was like the sun shining in its strength.

REVELATION 1:13-18 NASB

Sometimes you see something that is so awe-inspiring, you tremble. You might call it tremendous. Trembling is an autonomic response of the body to something which has overloaded the senses. The intensified emotions make the body shake.

How often do we actually experience this level of tremendous? The word has softened over time because now you can eat a sandwich and think it was tremendous. Really, though? Perhaps if you were rescued from the middle of the ocean after eleven traumatic days when you only had that sandwich to eat, it could rightly be labeled tremendous. You really would be shaking! God, revealed in his full glory, is tremendous.

What do these images of God in Scripture bring to mind?

Be Watchful

Be alert. Continue strong in the faith.
Have courage, and be strong. Do everything in love.

1 Corinthians 16:13-14 NCV

As adults, when we realize we are in a danger situation, we put ourselves on high alert. Have you ever walked through streets where you are clearly on the bad side of town, and you noticed people staring? Do you walk with your head down, unaware and unconcerned? No, your head is on a swivel, your body is tense, and you are in a heightened state of readiness, especially if you have your family with you. If you are in a group, you may be much more confident even though you are still aware.

As Christians, we are to be on high alert! We live in a dangerous season. We are engaged in a spiritual battle. Our lives are at risk and the enemy is looking to devour us. We are strengthened by gathering together with other believers. In this place with others who have a shared awareness, we have the best point of view. If something is missed by one of us, another sees it. There is safety in numbers.

How observant are you about what is happening in the world?

MADE RADIANT

We do see Him who was made for a little while lower than the angels, namely, Jesus, because of His suffering death crowned with glory and honor, so that by the grace of God He might taste death for everyone. For it was fitting for Him, for whom are all things, and through whom are all things, in bringing many sons to glory, to perfect the originator of their salvation through sufferings.

HEBREWS 2:9-10 NASB

As Adam led us into sin, Jesus leads us into righteousness. Sin brought with it brokenness and trouble; Jesus' righteousness brings healing and peace. But we do not yet have full freedom from this world, and just as Jesus willingly suffered for us, so too we are willing to suffer for him.

As Jesus was lowered to be a man in order to restore the creation to God, we also understand that we must lower ourselves to be witnesses for God. It is in this place, recognizing the trials we face, the humility we embrace, that God's grace becomes evident on the believer's face. The sons of glory are made radiant with his love.

Though you are called to lead, how do you show humility and grace?

UNRESTRAINED FESTIVITY

Break forth with dancing!
Make music and sing God's praises
with the rhythm of the drums!

PSALM 149:3 TPT

In many countries, people of differing ethnicities have fought bravely for liberty. If they can overcome their adversaries to the point of victory, there are spontaneous, exuberant responses. People do things without regard for social norms. The victorious will kiss strangers, fire their guns wildly, jump around unreservedly, and yell joyfully. When we claim victory over an oppressor whether on a smaller, personal level or on a larger scale, it calls for unrestrained festivities.

There will be a day when Jesus returns, and we will celebrate beyond our imaginations. Until that day comes, we will encounter smaller liberties, and they should also be celebrated. We should rejoice when we secure a victory over a besetting sin, when a loved one's illness is healed, or when we get an answer after months of prayer. Let us abandon shame-based restraints and let loose with exultations! Even though people may observe such responses with initially shocked, there is a mutual pleasure in seeing someone set free while openly expressing their gratitude to God.

When was the last time you were overjoyed and expressed it freely, even as a person in authority?

Delightful Moments

Since God has shown us great mercy, I beg you to offer your lives as a living sacrifice to him. Your offering must be only for God and pleasing to him.

ROMANS 12:1 NCV

The woman of the house had been away for a week, and she was looking forward to coming home to her husband and family. It had not been a successful trip, so her heart was a little heavy. She got home a little later than planned which only added to her frustration. When she opened the door, however, she was greeted by warm hugs and pleasurable aromas. The house smelled of a hot meal waiting to be shared. The family sat down to eat, and as they opened in prayer, she was even happier to be home. After the wonderful meal, the couple retired to the lounge and enjoyed talking about the week. As she fell asleep that night, she told Jesus this week didn't matter. Her heart was content with what she had.

Have you ever had those times when someone sacrificed themselves to allow you to have your needs met and for you to be happy? Those are such delightful moments in life.

What can you do to please someone in your life?

REALLY LISTENING

Let every person be quick to hear,
slow to speak.

JAMES 1:19 ESV

One of the hardest things for us to do is to truly listen to others. We like others to hear us. In God's Word, especially as you read through the book of Proverbs, he compels us to be quiet and listen. When we listen well and can respond with understanding words which reflect the true thoughts of the speaker, we confirm that we really do hear, and we validate what is being said. We hear and understand.

This is why reading God's Word aloud is a helpful activity. It pleases God for us to be reading, but when we speak it out, it helps us to hear it as well. As we equip others to accomplish God's plan for their lives, it is especially important for us to learn the art of listening well. Those we work with must be able to not only express their needs but also to feel that they are being heard. Are we not all in the same position with our God? He hears us well and meets our needs; we aspire to do the same for others.

How do you think listening to others affects how you listen to God?

A COOL BREEZE

"Repent of your sins and turn to God, so that your sins may
be wiped away. Then times of refreshment will come from
the presence of the Lord, and he will again send you Jesus,
your appointed Messiah."

ACTS 3:19-20 NLT

When you are working in the hot sun there will be a time
when it becomes unbearable. Your shirt is drenched with
sweat, you are covered in dirt, and the air is thick. The heat
saps your energy, and if you don't consume lots of liquids
you become dehydrated and dizzy. Eventually, you would
lose consciousness. When a cool breeze starts blowing,
it feels luxurious. It is so refreshing, especially if you can
enjoy a break in the shade and splash some cold water on
yourself.

This is what God wants for us. Our lives are full of good
things, but they can also be troublesome. We are in a battle,
and we're worn down and tired. God comes to us like a
fresh breeze and cool water. He gives us renewed strength
to continue the fight. Are you weary? Take a seat and wait
on God.

Can you feel God refreshing your soul?

No Explanation Needed

"Before I formed you in the womb I knew you,
before you were born I set you apart."

JEREMIAH 1:5 NIV

Have you ever worked with someone for so long that handing off jobs and tasks between you doesn't need explaining? They just take what you've done, do their part, and voila the project is complete. It makes life much easier when you are understood. It is also great to talk with friends when you don't always have to explain things. Sometimes you don't even have to talk; everything is known, understood, and implied.

Being understood comes from developing a closeness; God is immediately close and understanding, and he always welcomes us. He is right here with us. When we are understood, we feel accepted and appreciated. Each of us needs to be known, recognized, and accepted. This is how we understand love. God has declared that he knows, recognizes, and accepts us. When we find that perfect understanding in him, we also find the ability to make others feel understood.

How do you look to God for your need to be understood?
In what ways can that impact how you treat others?

THE CLOSEST FRIEND

"No longer do I call you servants, for the servant does not know what his master is doing; but I have called you friends, for all that I have heard from my Father I have made known to you."

JOHN 15:15 ESV

A friend can be closer than a brother, or a brother can be your closest friend. What drives these relationships is our ability to be vulnerable with one another and to allow trust bonds to form even when faced with difficulties. Friendships confront strain at times, but close camaraderie between two people can overcome troubles. It will even sometimes improve the relationship through those hardships. We find in these tough times that we are challenged to mature, especially in a close friendship. Good friends don't allow us to languish in remorse and pain, however, and try to help us find healing and wisdom.

Jesus says that he is also our good friend. This may strike us in different ways. Why would God be our friend? How can we be friends with God? It almost seems dishonoring because he is holy and righteous. But God, himself, calls us his friends and invites us to draw close to him in that special relationship.

How do you improve your friendships? Can you model that in your relationship with Christ?

Only Boast

Not that I have already obtained all this, or have already arrived at my goal, but I press on to take hold of that for which Christ Jesus took hold of me. Brothers and sisters, I do not consider myself yet to have taken hold of it. But one thing I do: Forgetting what is behind and straining toward what is ahead, I press on toward the goal to win the prize for which God has called me heavenward in Christ Jesus.

PHILIPPIANS 3:12-14 NIV

Paul wrote in the verses before today's verse that he placed no confidence in his own flesh. He had a strong testimony in saying this because, as far as following the Law went, he was faultless according in his day. He was an upstanding Pharisee who persecuted the church; he was a Hebrew of Hebrews. Yet, he said he could not boast about his earlier passion as a man of the Law. He was found wanting, lost in himself and in his own confidence.

When Christ set Paul straight, he realized that his only boast for good behavior and good works could be in the assurance of his faith in Jesus Christ. We also have some degree of self-confidence because of our leadership positions and our learned and acquired abilities, but Christ calls us to look only to him.

How do you embrace Christ's authority in your life despite the confidence people place in you to lead?

COMPARISON

In your relationships with one another, have the same mindset as Christ Jesus: Who, being in very nature God, did not consider equality with God something to be used to his own advantage; rather, he made himself nothing by taking the very nature of a servant, being made in human likeness… he humbled himself by becoming obedient to death.

PHILIPPIANS 2:5-8 NIV

It is in our nature to compare ourselves to others. When we do so, whomever we measure ourselves by provides the standard which then determines our status, at least in our own eyes. It is a very subjective human observance. We look at those who are worse to make ourselves feel better, or we look at those who are better and feel worse. What a terrible way to live.

Thank Jesus that we no longer have to compare ourselves to anyone! We, as believers, simply take on the nature of a servant of all regardless of who around us, and love everyone as Christ did. Christ liberated us and now our lives are reflected in the same servitude and humility that his was. At the right time, God will lift us up and we will be honored with those seated with Christ.

What do you need to do in order to avoid comparing yourself to others?

A Pragmatic Approach

"You naive ones, understand prudence;
And, you fools, understand wisdom!"

PROVERBS 8:5 NASB

The young investor had several close friends with whom he shared his stories. He told them about his successes at work and how it was benefiting his balance sheet. It wasn't pride; they were confidants. Eventually there was quite a nice sum of cash building up, and his friends had plenty to share about how they would use it. But the young man waited. He was careful and judicious. When the right moment arrived, he moved his cash into a security that more than doubled the value of the investment.

When we are prudent, life can be arduous; we deliberately take time to consider our ways and what we should do. When coupled with prayer and submitted to God, we learn the best way to manage our money as well as our attitude toward it. In general, we are supposed to pragmatically approach our planning for the future. God has an inheritance for us, so we also should be leaving an inheritance for those who come behind us. Prudent behavior allows us to focus on the more important legacy than possessions, which is demonstrating how to handle them.

What do your family and friends see exemplified in your life regarding the way you manage your finances?

Healthy Independence

The Lord is good to those who depend on him,
to those who search for him.
So it is good to wait quietly
for salvation from the Lord.

Lamentations 3:25-26 NLT

Healthy independence allows for people to coexist in stable relationships with contented hearts. When we find the freedom to express ourselves, to be okay with our weaknesses, and to be responsible for our own needs, we avoid placing these burdens on others. Our autonomy allows us to build strong bonds while avoiding unhealthy dependence in our relationships. Through this we understand our contributions and our gifts. We can appropriately see how our strengths fit uniquely in our teams and how they can benefit others. We also understand that their strengths cover our weaknesses.

Can we get to this level of self-actualization without the work of Christ in us? God encourages us to depend on him; our healthy independence requires dependence. Why? Because in this place our hearts can be rightly aligned with the one who made us and who knows all we need in order to be stable in our faith and content in our lives.

How can you depend on Christ in a way that reflects a healthy dependence on him?

Encouraging Fellowship

All Scripture is inspired by God and is useful for teaching,
for showing people what is wrong in their lives, for
correcting faults, and for teaching how to live right.

2 TIMOTHY 3:16 NCV

Some would say that the Bible is no longer relevant. It's true
that the Bible does not hold answers for every situation in
life. We also find that God has revealed truths in the Bible
about creation and about life in ancient cultures. However,
the Bible is critical and applicable in so many ways, none
more so than when we pray with the Word and listen to the
Holy Spirit. It is in this place that we find answers to life's
questions.

Also critical to our faith is the fellowship we find with other
believers. Our hearts are deceitful, and we can be led astray
even when we study the Word regularly. The reminder
and revealer for our own deception is often found in our
committed relationships to the people in our lives who also
pursue Christ. When we belong to a body of believers, the
blessings compound in terms of our own accountability
and our growth in the Spirit. Even with our workplace
friendships, we can encourage fellowship and study his
Word together.

*Are there ways you can encourage Scripture study with work
friends?*

GLORIOUS HANDIWORK

On the glorious splendor of your majesty,
and on your wondrous works, I will meditate.

PSALM 145:5 ESV

When we read Scripture, we find amazing descriptions about God. God is mysterious, powerful, wonderful, glorious, and holy. Sometimes he even elicits fear. It is very clear that God is majestic, and we can easily see evidence of his majesty in his creation. From the vast galaxies to the minute details of the animals, the birds, and the fish, his handiwork declares that he is God, and no one can compare to him.

All that is around us has been created by God simply by his spoken word. We also see what he has done through Christ; our salvation and our pending resurrection is testimony to his glory! He works in and through us continue to demonstrate the wonder of our God. He is worthy of our praise! We need to take time to stop and ponder who he is and all that he has made. We get busy and forget the incredible God we serve. Remember him today and what he is doing in you and the world around you at this very moment!

God's creation is glorious. What do you love about the wonder of the earth around you?

THE NEW EARTH

It is by his great mercy that we have been born again…
Now we live with great expectation, and we have a priceless
inheritance—an inheritance that is kept in heaven for you,
pure and undefiled, beyond the reach of change and decay.

1 PETER 1:3-4 NLT

God promises us eternity. We have an undying,
indestructible, unchanging inheritance in Christ. Not only
do we receive a lasting relationship with God, but we also
experience an everlasting and renewed earth. We are given
lasting bodies that do not deteriorate.

We get to be with each other forever. Praise God! This is
an amazing promise from our eternal Father. His presence
gives us great confidence to let go of life's concerns. We
can rest well knowing what he has in store for those whose
hearts are completely his. We can be excited about what our
future holds beyond this moment and this life!

*Have you thought about what your role might be in the new
earth? Does it make you excited about eternity?*

Making Peace

Since we have been justified by faith, we have peace with
God through our Lord Jesus Christ.

ROMANS 5:1 ESV

There is often a battle that rages within us when we
are accused of something we did not do. Whether we
misunderstood someone's comment or it was an intended
offense, our hackles are raised, and we begin to defend
ourselves. This is a natural response. Unfortunately it is
a common situation in the workplace. There are a lot of
different personalities and lifestyles that mix together in a
common work situation. It takes good leadership to step in
and make peace.

We are all guilty before God of creating a ruckus now and
then, and we are all in need of a peacemaker. We have no
leg to stand on when it comes to our own guilt, shame, and
depravity. There is no point trying to dispute this with God.
His response to our state is not one of condemnation but
of mercy, forgiveness, and grace. Through Jesus Christ, he
justifies us and vindicates us of all wrongdoing. All we have
to do is turn to him in repentance and submission; he is our
redeemer and our peacemaker.

When you sin, what helps you turn back to God and repent?

July

Remember your leaders who taught you the word of God. Think of all the good that has come from their lives, and follow the example of their faith.

Hebrews 13:7 NLT

The Right Judge

Whenever the LORD raised up a judge over Israel, he was with that judge and rescued the people from their enemies throughout the judge's lifetime. For the LORD took pity on his people, who were burdened by oppression and suffering.

JUDGES 2:18 NLT

The book of Judges covers the time period between the conquests of Joshua and the establishment of kings over Israel. God appointed wise leaders who established peace in the land. While the people were prudent and followed God, they had peace. Inevitably, however, they would choose independence from God, who would then not prevent surrounding nations from oppressing them. A new judge would then arise and through them God would liberate Israel. For years, the people vacillated between shrewd and senseless behavior.

They had several judges but eventually they demanded a king. Somehow they thought a king's discernment and wisdom would change their own behavior and minimize the opportunity for the neighboring countries to overcome them. But the kings acted no differently. A few of them did follow God, but for the most part Israel continued to suffer. Again God would have compassion on them. Eventually he sent his Son to rescue all of mankind.

Do you recognize the work of God's Spirit in your life?

INTENTIONAL SEEKING

"You will seek me and find me,
when you seek me with all your heart."

JEREMIAH 29:13 ESV

There is a caveat to the promise made in the verse today, and we can miss it if we read too quickly. If we seek God, will we find him? Not necessarily, not if we are apt to be careless about the way we search. God asks for us to be intentional when we seek him. We can't just turn up and hope that God's going to be present without much effort on our part. We need to come to him with our whole hearts.

Jacob wrestled all night with God, Moses climbed a mountain to meet up with him, and David spent countless hours praising the Almighty. This is the kind of gnawing hunger God wants us to demonstrate in our search for the truth. What does it take for us to show him this level of intentionality in our busy lives? We also have expectations from those we lead; do we want those people to show up without intending to exert some effort? Our time is precious, and God knows this, so moments of planned presence with him are critical. He loves it when we block time on our calendar for him. He has called us into our roles and has grace for us to find ways to wholeheartedly seek him.

What do you do to set aside quality time with God?

TRANQUILITY

Surrender your anxiety.
Be still and realize that I am God.
I am God about all the nations,
and I am exalted throughout the whole earth.

PSALM 46:10 TPT

The businesswoman loved hiking. Getting out of the office was a surreal experience after a heavy week. The mountains loomed high above her, capped with black cliffs frosted in white snow. The sun was bright, and the sky was blue; the bright reflections created sapphire-colored light that shimmered in the stream. Birds chirped in the green canopy above while squirrels tussled in the leaves below. She loved these moments of tranquility with no one around: just nature at its best and the Creator by her side. She found in these times that stillness returned to her soul. The worries of work and life drifted away, and she felt a soothing rhythm in the relaxing sounds of nature.

There is great peace in God's creation. When we take some time away from our harried lives and enter into the stillness of God's rest, a serene peace washes over us. We can rest in him.

Where do you go to meet with God and find peace?

FIGHT FOR FREEDOM

It was for freedom that Christ set us free;
therefore keep standing firm and do not be subject again
to a yoke of slavery.

GALATIANS 5:1 NASB

"Freedom!" was cried out by many as they were led away to be slaughtered. In the name of liberty, men and women have died. It does not matter the country, the ethnicity, or the region, people have fought for freedom, and they will continue to do so. Humans were not made to be slaves to anyone but God. We were made to enjoy our Father and to walk freely with him. He created us to live with each other in peace and unity. We were made to be joyful in our lives and in our Creator.

We trap ourselves into being subject to things without realizing it. We become slaves to our sins, habits, money, work, possessions, people, religion, regulations, or governments. These are just a few of the things which we allow to become our masters. Christ provided us freedom from all enslavements. We receive in him a freedom for which he died. Now we can choose to not sin; we have a new and complete freedom to love each other and to love him. Stand firm in your faith today and be liberated through him.

How can you bring grateful thoughts of God into your mind in your day-to-day life?

A Firm Foundation

Your faithfulness endures to all generations;
you have established the earth, and it stands fast.

PSALM 119:90 ESV

One of the great comforts of knowing God is found in his character. He is perfectly faithful. There is no wavering, no need to question his decisions, and no concern that he will not do that which he said he would do. He is enduring. His promises will never fail. What he has said will come to pass no matter how long it takes. He is patient. He is not in a hurry and will wait for us to come to the right place and mindset. He is not overwhelmed by chaos. He is gracious.

Knowing that we are weak and his strength can compensate for all of us creates a firm foundation. His perfection replaces our failures. His steady, faithful, enduring, patient, and gracious character is our strength. Through this knowledge and our repentance, we are established as his children, and we can bravely face the world with confidence. Because of his character we can stand fast.

What about God brings you comfort in the midst of chaos?

HAPPINESS OF GOD

I realize that the best thing for them is to be happy and enjoy themselves as long as they live. God wants all people to eat and drink and be happy in their work, which are gifts from God.

ECCLESIASTES 3:12-13 NCV

What is it about God that he wants people to be happy? He does, and though you may resist the thought, happiness is a part of God's kingdom. It's not fake and it's not temporary. We will continue to experience it into eternity. We know the angry God, the just God, the loving God, and the gracious God, but do we know the happy God? Have we got a roadblock in our mind that God is not happy?

From a human perspective, happiness contains multiple dimensions tied to meaningfulness, healthy relationships, a broad spectrum of experiences, and a healthy work-life balance. Are these not things that God wants for us too? Does he have these in full himself? Yes, God is happy. This does not exclude his other emotions, but we can think of him as happy.

What picture do you get when you think of God as happy?

FOCUSED TIME

Certainly God has heard me;
He has attended to the voice of my prayer.

PSALM 66:19 NKJV

Being fully engaged in what you are doing is rewarding. Having the time and freedom to completely focus your attention on a subject or activity allows for a greater chance for good productivity. The positive feelings which occur because of better production brings pleasure from endorphins being released. When this is added to having healthy relationships and good team camaraderie, there exists a great scenario for an enjoyable work environment.

We were created to engage in tasks and to enjoy our relationships. We were made for companionship at home, work, church, and in leisure. It ties directly to our Creator's command which gives us dominion over the earth to care for it and to be creative together. As we think about focused times we have had in the past, consider how God is listening attentively to our prayers. He loves us deeply and wants to converse with us. He desires to connect so he hears whatever we share with him.

How does it feel when you are with someone, and they are attentive to you?

HONORING MARRIAGE

Love must be sincere. Hate what is evil;
cling to what is good.

ROMANS 12:9 NIV

Our society has morally collapsed in the realm of sexuality.
We worship at the foot of Aphrodite, gobbling up her
lavish impurity. Infidelity is common, divorce is rampant,
perversion is celebrated, and pornography rages. Sex
slavery and human trafficking is increasing across the
globe. Millions of women and children are being sold and
imprisoned for the pleasure of others and the monetary
benefit of people who have robbed them of their rights.
People have been groomed to feed lust with a multiplicity
of electronic devices. God forgive us. At the same time and
as a direct result of this activity, we see the dishonoring of
marriage and a generation disenchanted with the concept
of creating a bond before God which is not to be broken.
People wonder why a right-minded individual would ever
marry. It is an archaic institution, right? What does a piece
of paper mean anymore?

God created man and woman to be bonded together once
and for life. We are not animals, but we have become
frighteningly similar to them in our basal behavior sexually.
We must get back to honoring each other in the pure love
of God and with his life-honoring intentions.

How are you honoring marriage?

FLEXIBILITY

When I am with those who are weak, I share their
weakness, for I want to bring the weak to Christ.
Yes, I try to find common ground with everyone,
doing everything I can to save some.

1 CORINTHIANS 9:22 NLT

Contortionists do things that we think are not humanly
possible. They bend their bodies and fit into objects that
make most of us cringe. Contortionists develop this talent
by learning and practicing. They keep their bodies flexible.

Our mental flexibility is also important. Throughout our
lives the flexibility of our brains, called neuroplasticity, is
reinforced by learning and experiencing new things. We
may not be able to learn as quickly as we once did, but our
experiences teach us how to learn effectively. Maintaining
the ability to acquire new skills and knowledge in our
roles is critical to staying current and staying healthy.
Doing new things and meeting new people helps us grow
in understanding and wisdom so we don't stagnate in an
inflexible life.

*As you consider flexibility, have you thought about outreach
opportunities or missions?*

PREPARED TO SURVIVE

With minds that are alert and fully sober, set your hope on the grace to be brought to you when Jesus Christ is revealed at his coming.

1 PETER 1:13 NIV

The difference between being prepared or not can turn a simple bout of bad weather into a life-or-death situation. If you have ever been caught in a thunderstorm when the temperature drops suddenly and heavy rains and strong winds develop, you know what this means. The right equipment—additional warm layers, rain gear, and the right footwear—allows you to endure a sudden storm with minor issues. When you are exposed and ill prepared, however, it becomes a matter of survival.

Proper preparedness is not only important when we work, travel, camp, or live our day-to-day lives; it is important in our faith. How are we ready for whatever we may face as political climates change, or as people turn against Christians? Many believers around the world experience this right now. We are promised resurrection, but trouble will occur before the final redemption. Let us get ready!

How can you prepare your faith and encourage those around you to do the same?

A CENTERED LIFE

A man of kindness attracts favor,
while a cruel man attracts nothing but trouble.

PROVERBS 11:17 TPT

Being self-aware and demonstrating authenticity are core qualities to being a poised person. The word calls to mind someone who is self-assured and approaches life with balance and grace. Decisions are deliberate and thoughtful, but passion is utilized when the moment calls for it.

Sounds like Jesus, doesn't it? He had all of these traits and more. Though he may not have been physically attractive to draw people to him according to Isaiah 53:2, he attracted them to himself because of his persona. He was dignified and secure, so people also felt assured when they were around him. The poised leader provides security which comes from a centered life. Believers' lives are focused and intentionally connected to Jesus. This allows us to provide security and strength to others which we may not even recognize. It is a joy that God uses us to draw people to himself. We can be encouraged to know that even when we may fail to be kind, he gives us grace and compassion which allows us to love others well.

Do others feel secure around you?

LEARN TO ENDURE

We also glory in tribulations, knowing that tribulation
produces perseverance; and perseverance, character;
and character, hope.

ROMANS 5:3-4 NKJV

One foot in front of the other. That's what the soldier had
to do in order to keep going. If he was going to make it
through, he had to be stubbornly resolute. He was not
going to stop moving. His commission was clear: if he did
not get the message across, men would die. Through enemy
territory, even though he was injured and lost, he tirelessly
trudged on. There was no one else to do this; he had to
endure, and he could not stop.

Many of us have not faced war. We are very thankful to
those who have. They have learned to endure through
trials we have not faced and cannot imagine. They paid a
price which has provided our freedom. In our troubles, it is
helpful to acquire an accurate perspective. Are we bleeding?
Are we stressed to the point of death? Most often we are in
safe places, and we have good resources around us. We only
need to reach out to God and others, and help will be there.

Which of your friends or co-workers help you endure?

CONSIDER NATURE

"Notice how the lilies of the field grow; they do not labor nor do they spin thread for cloth, yet I say to you that not even Solomon in all his glory clothed himself like one of these. But if God so clothes the grass of the field, which is alive today and tomorrow is thrown into the furnace, will He not much more clothe you?"

MATTHEW 6:28-30 NASB

Jesus says to *consider nature*. Look at what is happening around you and you will see God in it. How does he take care of the sparrow and the flower? God is active in our lives and involved in the details far beyond what we realize. Yes, we are that important to him, even down to the number of hairs on our heads. Would the Father send the Son to die for that which he did not deem critical? He would not. He could easily have left us to our own demise. It would not have taken long. And then he could have started over.

What we witness in the world is a God who views us as his own. He created us and came to us. We have been well regarded by him and that should cause us to be mindful of him in both nature and in his people.

What do you see of God in nature and people that you can be thankful for today?

SHELTER IN THE STORM

In the depths of my heart I truly know
that you, Yahweh, have become my Shield;
You take me and surround me with yourself.
Your glory covers me continually.
You lift high my head.

PSALM 3:3 TPT

It was early in the morning, and the boy awoke to the flash of lightning and the clap of thunder. He felt the house rumble and heard the rain splattering on the rooftop. The tin roof created a rhythmic sound that lulled him back to sleep. Snuggled up in his warm blanket, he slept the storm away and then awakened a second time to his mother's voice calling him to breakfast.

In the middle of a great storm, it is such a comfort to be with family inside a warm house and a cozy bed. It's pure luxury to be protected from the elements and insulated by love. This is the provision God has for us all. His love is no different when he covers us. He forgives us for our sins, and he welcomes us into his family. His love lifts our eyes to him, and we are sheltered.

Why does God want to be with us?

SAFEGUARDS

It is not for kings, Lemuel—
it is not for kings to drink wine,
not for rulers to crave beer,
lest they drink and forget what has been decreed,
and deprive all the oppressed of their rights.

PROVERBS 31:4-5 NIV

It is easy for leaders to become overwhelmed with all that is going on. And sometimes this can lead to a momentary lapse in judgment that causes them to indulge in some form of revelry that is not appropriate to the position. For Christians, we can thank God for his grace and forgiveness when we become sidelined by some form of overindulgence. But when sin is ongoing and it becomes a craving, the warning in today's verse makes it clear that the people will suffer. People here means those who directly work for a leader or are influenced by them. We have seen this happen, and we know the trajectory of those who fall prey to addictions or even bad habits.

What safeguards have we put in place for ourselves if temptations become problematic and entrenched in our lives? Are we isolated, or have we surrounded ourselves with mentors and advisors who will lovingly hold us accountable and be there on the path back?

Can you reach out to a fellow leader and check in with each other?

RECOUNT AND RECONCILE

All this is from God, who through Christ reconciled us to himself and gave us the ministry of reconciliation.

2 CORINTHIANS 5:18 ESV

Coming home to those you love and who love you is a delight. How great it is to reconnect with a loved one after a long period of absence. Words never seem to suffice. Most often the smile on the face and the warmth of the embrace is all that is needed. After that initial connection time, there's conversations and reminiscing about times spent together as well as during the absence.

How opposite this is to reconciliation when much of the conversing and recounting needs to happen first. With good peacemaking, there are often tears, and hopefully, an embrace. What starts out as a situation with strong negative emotions is then resolved in peace and hopefulness. What a joy those times are to the soul. It is like something is set free within. With God, our reconciliation is similar. We need his Word, we need to recount our sins, and then we are reconciled to him through Christ and because of our repentance. He humbled himself to bring us into a right relationship with him.

Do you need to humble yourself to reconcile with anyone?

CONTROLLING CHAOS

"God is not man, that he should lie,
or a son of man, that he should change his mind.
Has he said, and will he not do it?
Or has he spoken, and will he not fulfill it?"

NUMBERS 23:19 ESV

So many things happen in this life that create chaos.
There is a deviation here and there, or a block in the road.
Sometimes we have to handle a disruption of plans, or a
death or some other form of disaster. Even the wonder of a
new life presents its own special chaos. We try as much as
we can to make order out of disorder, but the older we get
the better we understand that control is only temporary. At
least it's a worthy goal in life to hopefully get to a place of
understanding this truth and being able to live with it.

Where does our stability in life lay? If we cannot control
chaos, does chaos control us? That is always the fear that
grips the heart of all leaders. We need security and stability.
We need something that is changeless so we can remain
anchored to something. But we also need the changes
because in between chaos and control is real, vibrant,
exciting life.

*Christ is your security when you go through chaos. How do
you look to him?*

Sneaky Sins

Do not love the world or the things in the world. If anyone
loves the world, the love of the Father is not in him. For all
that is in the world—the desires of the flesh and the desires
of the eyes and pride of life—is not from the Father but is
from the world. And the world is passing away along with
its desires, but whoever does the will of God abides forever.

1 John 2:15-17 ESV

If we want to be shepherds of people, we must be alert to
the three distracting temptations that are in today's verse.
These sneaky sins can enter into our hearts unless we pray
against them. John writes that they are not from the Father.
Desires of the flesh are our urgings and yearnings which are
not from the Holy Spirit. Desires of the eyes means to covet
what we do not have. The pride of life is whatever feeds our
over-inflated egos and our desire for control. Which one
hits us the hardest?

We are all troubled by some or all of these sins, yet God
has delivered us from being slaves to them. We no longer
walk through our day blind to our own depravity. We are
awakened by the urging and teaching of the Holy Spirit. He
wants to be with us, and we want to be with him. This is a
result of the work within us which draws us away from the
sins listed above.

Why do you want to please God?

KEEP YOUR WORD

We must be those who never need to verify our speech as truthful by swearing by the heavens or the earth or any other oath. But instead we must be so full of integrity that our "Yes" or "No" is convincing enough and we do not stumble into hypocrisy.

JAMES 5:12 TPT

When a person has a deadline and they have consistently shown themselves capable of meeting in the past, do we doubt them? No, we would even say *when they say it, they mean it*. We are confident in their word. That is a big deal spiritually, emotionally, and mentally. God made promises in his Word, and because of who he is, we can trust him implicitly. He said it, so he meant it. It will happen.

As believers, we want to emulate him in our commitments to others. Knowing ourselves and overcoming our sinful tendencies in keeping our word is very important as children of God. If we procrastinate or tend to be late, we need to take this into consideration so we can give our word with integrity. We have been given the position of leader, and in part this would be because of our ability to keep our word. Let us keep that up!

How can you improve your commitment to keeping your word?

GENTLENESS IN FAILURE

May you always be filled with the fruit of your salvation—
the righteous character produced in your life by Jesus
Christ—for this will bring much glory and praise to God.

PHILIPPIANS 1:11 NLT

There is something pleasant about gentleness in a person.
It's the look of a mother holding a newborn babe, a father
helping his child up from a fall, or the face of Jesus as
he held out his hand to the woman caught in adultery.
These are all pictures of gentleness in action. It is the kind,
calming act that soothes and helps us in a time of difficulty.

How do we demonstrate this behavior in our workplaces
when people fail and make mistakes? It is a difficult
situation because we don't want to lower quality or reduce
productivity. We do want people to be kind to one another,
however, and we want to be kind to others too. We need to
be people of character who can be gracious while dealing
with errors, yet strong when completing what needs to be
accomplished. That is what we witness in the person of Jesus.

How are you gentle with those around you?

GET AFTER IT

Do not be slothful in zeal,
be fervent in spirit,
serve the Lord.

ROMANS 12:11 ESV

On its own, this verse can seem rather abrasive. *Don't be so lazy; pick yourself up and get to serving the Lord already.* But in context of the whole chapter, it is actually encouraging us to honor and love one another with zeal and fervor as Christ has loved us. The last part of the verse is important. What can we really do to serve the Lord? Does he need things from us? That is unlikely.

God wants us to serve him by loving and honoring others. This lightens the burden for us as we know he promises in multiple ways to provide all we need and to sustain us consistently. His passion and purpose for the collective good is far greater than ours. We can be confident we will be well provisioned but getting after it and being obedient falls on us. Let us find ways to outdo one another with good works of lovingkindness.

How can you go over and above for your team today?

GUIDE TO TRUTH

Be wise as to what is good
and innocent as to what is evil.

ROMANS 16:19 ESV

The little girl was missing from the fun. Her name was called over and over, but to no avail. Eventually she was discovered hiding from the others and missing out on the party games. Her face and hands, however, were smothered in chocolate. She was gorging herself on it, and her innocent face showed her shame. Had she done wrong? Not really, but she thought she had. After some assurance and a wipe down, she was off playing again with her friends. She was only two, and it was a birthday party after all.

We can be like this child with no way to decipher between good and evil. Sometimes it's because we choose not to properly discern, feigning ignorance but really just engaging in our own selfishness. Other times we are caught in circumstances we don't understand but legitimately feel shame even though we ought not to. And then there are times when we are unaware of how we got into the middle of a situation, and we need wisdom. God's Word is our only guide to the truth in this ever-shifting world. Our connection to the Holy Spirit is the key to discerning between good and evil.

How do you determine what is evil and what is good?

MEASURING SUCCESS

"I have come down from heaven, not to do My own will,
but the will of Him who sent Me."

JOHN 6:38 NKJV

Feeling successful is an important part of being human. We
want to have something we can do to feel accomplished.
No person should feel purposeless. The critical point
for success is understanding what we consider to be
the method of measuring success. What makes one
feel successful? Is it the praise of other men? Are we
accomplishing what we think should be done? Is the goal
meaningful to us? Or do we hear whatever it is that God
deems as important, so when we do it, we find success?

There are many ways to approach the concept of success,
but ultimately only one person decides if we are successful
or not, and that is God. What does he measure our success
by? Jesus said that doing the will of the Father is our only
requirement for success. We need to not tie success to any
human institution or measurement. God's will is that we
obey his Spirit.

How can you improve your ability to listen to the Holy Spirit?

OLD HURTS

As high as the heavens are above the earth,
so great is his love for those who fear him;
as far as the east is from the west,
so far has he removed our transgressions from us.

PSALM 103:11-12 NIV

What does it take to forgive someone? It is not about putting something on a shelf and forgetting about it or releasing it to the wind. Forgiveness is about choosing not to remember. That is what God does. He chooses to not recount our sins. He doesn't put them on a top shelf in a vain effort to forget. With all humanity's sin, his shelves would break! Who could even count their many sins against God? As he forgives us, he asks us to forgive others.

This takes a lot of heart-level effort because we all want justice. We have feelings, thoughts, and scars that need healing. We can also experience a similar offense that triggers a past experience, so all those old, unforgiven hurts come rushing back! Like Christ, we have to put our hope in the one who judges justly. We have to extend grace, knowing he will make things right one day.

Can you take time today to forgive someone by naming how you were hurt by them and asking Christ to help you?

UNQUESTIONABLE

May God give you more and more grace and peace as you
grow in your knowledge of God and Jesus our Lord.

2 PETER 1:2 NLT

When we question the meaning of life we usually end up
at God's doorstep. But not always. Some people end up in
some dark place of hopelessness or searching through the
tenets of some self-actualizing practice. Others look into
religions that partially imitate God's truth but miss the real
point. At some stage we have to wrestle with the existence
of God, whether he is perfect or fallible, and whether or not
he is in control of this chaos.

We should question these things. Any Christian worth his
salt asks and wonders about the bigger issues in life. When
people tell you not to question, that is a sign to be cautious.
God can handle our questions. Man is the one who worries
about how they will be answered. God wants us to come
to him with our concerns and not to hide them. Thomas
doubted and Jesus welcomed him to speak the truth about
those doubts. He made himself real in the way that Thomas
needed. God has strong character. When we realize he does
not deviate from who he is, the answers often come to us.

What are the characteristics of God that you love?

SHOCKING

In your glory and grandeur go forth in victory!
Through your faithfulness and meekness
the cause of truth and justice will stand.
Awe-inspiring miracles are accomplished by your power,
leaving everyone dazed and astonished!

PSALM 45:4 TPT

Have you ever been electrocuted? How about being shocked enough to stop everything. Perhaps you can recall an incident that caused time to stand still. Suddenly, your mouth was agape, and your eyes were wide with wonder. These occurrences were likely not from electricity! Maybe you were shocked by some news you received, watching a sporting event, or even by something that was so very beautiful. Or you may have been stunned by a painful experience or a joyous occasion.

There are many moments in life when we experience shock. The good experiences come from fresh surprises or good discoveries. For successful teamwork, it is important to integrate creativity and adventure into our routines. We were made to be more than robots repeating safe habits. As we allow for new experiences and the possibility of encountering stunning moments, we find fresh value in work and life.

What new moment can you create for those you work with?

AFFIRMED WITH AFFECTION

The LORD set his affection on your ancestors and loved
them, and he chose you, their descendants,
above all the nations as it is today.

DEUTERONOMY 10:15 NIV

When we come to realize that a good Father created us,
and we accept that he truly loves us, we can enjoy a secure
relationship with God. Most of us are not Jewish as many
believers were in biblical times, but we are now blended
into his family as he intended. We accept that he has
chosen us. We can wonder why, but ultimately embracing
God's affection anchors us in our relationship with him.
It is his goodness that does this, not our worth. It is his
righteousness that allows it, not our good behavior. It is his
love that overcomes all obstacles, not our righteous hearts.

As we ponder his love and affection, we come to
understand that there is not anything we can do before a
holy God to make ourselves worthy. He is great and we are
but dust, yet he values us beyond our understanding of his
creation and the wonders of his universe.

Can you accept God's affection for you?

REASON TO BE THANKFUL

A joyful heart is good medicine,
but a broken spirit dries up the bones.

PROVERBS 17:22 CSB

Have you ever spent time working alongside someone who always complains? It can truly wear a person out. There is no joy in being with those who grumble about their lives and whine about their circumstances. We give allowances for people going through dark times, and we definitely want to be there for them knowing they would similarly be present for us. Once the difficulty is over, however, there is blessing in spending time with someone who has a positive outlook. It brings healing to the soul.

Positivity comes from finding a reason to be thankful in any situation. Being positive is not for the fainthearted because it is easy to be one who complains. Life is full of bad times. What can we do differently? As Paul wrote in today's verse, it is the state of being thankful in all things that enables a person to overcome extraordinary situations. Likely none of us have been through what Paul experienced, yet he called us to thankfulness. If he could do it, so can we.

What are you able to change in your response to difficult situations? What would help you to be thankful?

THE "EST"

"Blessed are those who trust in the LORD
and have made the LORD their hope and confidence."

Some favored people seem to have the sun shining on them all the time. They seem to walk through life being treated with preference. The rain never falls on them; they have nothing but blue skies. Rules do apply to them, but they are somewhat flexible, far more than for most of us who live under a heavy hand. When favored people break the rules, there seems to be some special application of justice exclusive to them. It is not because they are special people. They are not the strongest, smartest, tallest, or any other "est." They just seem to be blessed. We see these favored ones at work—even on our teams—and we smile and shake our heads when we think of them.

Christians are favored. God smiles upon us. We are treated with preference by God; legalistic rules wash away as we are led by the Spirit. When we fail, our special justice is Christs righteousness. It is not because we are above others. We aren't the *est* of anything. It is because God especially chose us. We are his children, and that means we are favored.

How does being favored by God help you to love others? How can that help you bless your team?

PATIENT DISCERNMENT

"Your servant is in the midst of Your people whom
You have chosen, a great people who are too many
to be numbered or counted. So give Your servant an
understanding heart to judge Your people, to discern
between good and evil. For who is capable of judging this
great people of Yours?"

1 KINGS 3:8-9 NASB

Discernment requires patience and wisdom as we search
out what is happening behind the scenes. Solomon knew
that so many people needed his attention, so he would need
help. He could not see behind the scenes on his own, so he
asked for God's Spirit to give him wisdom. His rulership and
success were built on his dependence upon the Holy Spirit.

Our abilities to lead well also requires us to lean into God's
Spirit. How do we do this? We take time to listen to him.
We stay close to God by praying and reading the Word
hungrily. We don't rush our people or our decisions, and
we are patient because the Spirit helps us to be so. He is
actively speaking to us throughout the day, and we only
have to listen and follow as Jesus did.

What can you do to improve your discernment?

CAREFUL AND WISE

Be very careful how you live.
Do not live like those who are not wise,
but live wisely.

EPHESIANS 5:15 NCV

Being careful can be born out of fear or indecision, but it can also be founded in vigilance and necessary caution. As believers in Christ, our wariness should be against becoming lethargic and distracted by so many vices. If we are not alert, we can easily fall prey to a mediocre form of Christianity which has no power. Our power comes from the Holy Spirit. Wisdom, vigilance, and other qualities which build our carefulness also come from him.

Paul wrote that we should live wisely and carefully; he encourages us to be filled with the Holy Spirit so we can actually do so. Our daily tasks involve a dependence on the Spirit, our time at home involves him, and our evenings involve him. Even in our sleep he speaks to us. He is with us always. Our recognition and intentional invitation to listen to him throughout our day is important to living a wisdom-filled, guarded life. He gives us the skills we need to be careful and wise.

In what state do you want Jesus to find you when he returns?
How will you get there?

August

God blesses those who patiently endure testing and temptation. Afterward they will receive the crown of life that God has promised to those who love him.

James 1:12 NLT

SEEKING GUIDANCE

*He guides the humble in what is right
and teaches them his way.*

PSALM 25:9 NIV

Starting a business or organization is stressful. There is no secret sauce to make it work each time an attempt is made. A new start-up owner needs people who have good counsel and a vision to see all the angles. It requires labor, diligence, perseverance, and fortitude. That is an excellent list of attributes so it could be the secret sauce! The most important indicator which increases the opportunity for success, however, is the ability to listen to those wise counselors. Humility is the wisdom that the owners of new ventures really need so they can hear the guidance given to them.

The Bible is clear that wise counsel allows success. It does, however, require that the counseled one listen and observe. It is a good thing to rely on others to guide decisions and to open up the best chances for the best outcome. We value the perspective of the Holy Spirit, and his wisdom is pure and right. May we have ears to hear.

Who do you seek when you need wise counsel?

Happiness High

Make sure that your character is free from the love of money,
being content with what you have; for He Himself has said,
"I will never desert you, nor will I ever abandon you."

Hebrews 13:5 nasb

True happiness is found in contentment. There are solid
steps a believer can take to allow us to be thankful for what
we have and not desiring what we don't have. It is found in
pursuing healthy relationships where we are loved for who
we actually are and not what we do or how we do it.

We often search for happiness in the wrong places
or the wrong ways. We seek thrills with possessions,
entertainment, or the wrong relationships. True
happiness is not found in the constant release of the
happiness hormones—dopamine, serotonin, oxytocin,
and endorphins. These are experiential highs which are
hormonally released through activities. Although happiness
does involve these hormones, when a healthy form of
happiness is achieved, they are the result. They should
not be the goal. Happiness is found in being content with
what you have, not comparing yourself to others, and not
searching for hormonally heightened experiences.

What do you enjoy about your life?

Thinking Pattern

Whatever is true, whatever is honorable, whatever is just, whatever is pure, whatever is lovely, whatever is commendable, if there is any excellence, if there is anything worthy of praise, think about these things.

PHILIPPIANS 4:8 ESV

We are of the age when we practice metacognition. This is the awareness of our own thoughts and the appropriate analysis of them. We are also probably aware of our thinking habits. We all get stuck in certain thinking patterns which tend to maintain our worldviews, influence our actions, and trigger our emotions.

Paul wrote in the book of Romans that we are to renew our minds. It's a command, not a request, and he is confident that we can do it because Christ has liberated us from darkness. We have control over our thoughts. He encourages us to think noble thoughts. We are told to dwell on decency, virtue, justice, and purity. We purposefully seek to have honorable thoughts and steer toward excellence and praiseworthiness. We want to be mature in our thought life and to recognize what we are thinking and where change is needed. When our minds are positive, pure, and loving God, it changes our countenance and our actions toward everyone around us at work and at home.

What would change for you if you were to dwell upon all good things?

COMPELLING FOR GOOD

Christ's love compels us, because we are convinced that one died for all, and therefore all died. And he died for all, that those who live should no longer live for themselves but for him who died for them and was raised again.

2 CORINTHIANS 5:14-15 NIV

The man attested to his innocence and tried to explain to the authorities that what happened wasn't his fault. His friend had done the deed and then convinced him to go look at it. Out of curiosity he went, and when the authorities came, he was implicated. Have you ever had one of those friends? Perhaps you were the one who got people excited to do questionable things and then stepped back. Perhaps you were the friend who was very persuasive.

Persuasiveness can be used for good or bad. As believers, we rely on the teachings and nudging of the Spirit to compel us toward good. Jesus was fascinating, compelling, and good. His disciples set their things down and followed him because of the beautiful and compelling call to go with him. Similarly, we have given up sin and its many tempting pleasures to follow him. We are even willing to lay down our lives in the service and sacrifice for him! There is no more compelling friend, and he will never let you down.

What convinced you to follow Christ?

PRECEDING REPUTATION

Never let loyalty and kindness leave you…
Write them deep within your heart.
Then you will find favor with both God and people,
and you will earn a good reputation.

PROVERBS 3:3-4 NLT

The reputation of a person is often known before ever meeting them. *Their reputation precedes them.* It can be earned for various things like excellence, trustworthiness, humor, or strategy. Sometimes, though, a reputation demonstrates negative characteristics like greed, anger, impatience, or arrogance. People who behave badly end up with a bad reputation. Being reputable means to be highly regarded by others. People see a reputable person as having sound judgment, honest speech, and dependability in their deeds. We are necessarily burdened with the requirement of a good reputation as leaders.

When you think of your friends or close acquaintances who have good reputations, what characterizes them? Like Jesus, those you relate to likely have some good characteristics to notice and appreciate. Perhaps you are drawn to things you see in yourself that you value in those around you. The Bible talks about bad morals corrupting the good, but the opposite can also true: those with good morals encourage respectable behavior if they keep their eyes on Jesus and their hearts in the Word.

What reputation precedes you?

EDIFYING WORDS

Let us pursue the things which make for peace
and the things by which one may edify another.

ROMANS 14:19 NKJV

God's Word tells us that from our mouths come the matters
of the heart. When our words and jokes get out of hand,
we risk erasing the work that the Spirit has done on our
behalf as a testimony to the Lord. It can happen pretty
quickly if we are speaking without thinking. When we
hold our tongues, we start to notice maturity developing in
ourselves. It's a beautiful thing when we take time before
saying something unedifying and purposefully choose
better words.

As men and women of faith we desire to enrich each
other's lives. We want to encourage one another in our
faith. We also have to consider what that looks like in our
workplaces. So often gossip, slander, and lude jokes can
burden and discourage us. It is helpful if we seek God, are
filled with grace, and speak his truth. Out of this posture we
can lead others into a God-centered dialogue that edifies
one another.

How can you seek God more in your daily life?

PLEASURE OF PEOPLE

He causes the grass to grow for the cattle,
And vegetation for the labor of mankind,
So that they may produce food from the earth,
And wine, which makes a human heart cheerful,
So that he makes his face gleam with oil,
And food, which sustains a human heart.

PSALM 104:14-15 NASB

Think of those times you had a feast of a meal, a celebratory occasion. What is on the table? Who is with you? Picture all those foods you love, drinks you enjoy, and the best company with whom to share it. This is excellent! It is marvelous!

There are many excellent things in our lives which we can enjoy, but nothing is more exceptional than good company and delicious food and drink. It is a shared pleasure of people from all over the world in all ethnicities and all generations. In fact, it is so excellent that at the end of all things, God gathers all his people for a massive celebration with great food and drink.

Can you invite friends over this week to share some food and drink and celebrate God together?

STEADY PATH

All the paths of the LORD are steadfast love and faithfulness,
for those who keep his covenant and his testimonies.

PSALM 25:10 ESV

Many of us walk a lot. It's a big part of what humans do. But have you ever walked on a path where it is difficult to be surefooted because it is so rocky? It is tough to stay balanced, especially if you are carrying anyone or anything. If the path is slippery from rain, it's a recipe for injury. This is what happens to the person who walks in their own strength, independent from God.

On that same path, if there is a rope tethered to the cliff which you can take hold of, you will be more stable. If you have a wise friend to go with you to point out difficulties and to share your load, the journey is vastly improved. You are guided, supported, and strengthened. This is the path of those who keep God's Word. He is the steadfast and faithful friend who helps carry your load, guides you through tough spots, and catches you when you fall.

What troubles have you gone through recently where you saw God's faithfulness?

MEEK OR WEAK

"Blessed are the meek,
for they shall inherit the earth."

MATTHEW 5:5 ESV

Does meek mean weak? Must the meek turn the other cheek? In the upside-down-inside-out kingdom of God, the way of Jesus was not seen as weak. Meekness in Jesus was strength, righteousness, and truth. The Holy Spirit spoke through Jesus the Words of truth and life that pierced the darkness and destroyed Satan's strongholds. So even though he did not fight physically, nor did he did not lash out cruelly, he was gentle and loving. He was also not quiet when it suited God's purposes, such as when he cleared the temple of the buyers and sellers before the Passover when he was crucified.

We tend to fight for our own pride. God works in the believer's heart when we get like this and sometimes, we respond poorly when we feel our rights are being offended. We may say that we don't deserve to be treated badly, and we might even be right. But does arguing suit God's purposes, or are we serving our own? It is clear that God rewards those who follow his ways. The meek will inherit the earth, not the ones concerned about their own reputation and pride.

How do you strive to put aside your ego in order to better serve God's purposes?

FILLED WITH PRAISE

How could I be silent when it's time to praise you?
Now my heart sings out, bursting with joy—
a bliss inside that keeps me singing,
"I can never thank you enough!"

PSALM 30:12 TPT

God's creation is astounding. It is hard to put into words what we see in nature throughout the day and as the seasons change. We find ourselves speechless when we are not expecting something, and it is suddenly upon us. We see a marvelous view from a high point, or an athlete performs an astounding feat; we're at a concert and a talented musician moves heaven and earth with an amazing song, or a beloved spouse looks stunning and there's nothing like that feeling when we look at them.

However it happens, when we are blown away by something God made and when we truly grasp that he made it, we want to shout out his praises. We don't applaud his creation with a light clap; our exultation rises to the Creator with great gusto. He is the one deserving of worship. Whatever takes our breath away will result in us glorifying the one who gave us that breath! That is the joy and celebration that we have for him. He is incredible! We love his handiwork and thank him for it. We love you, Jesus!

How do you see God in his creation, and what fills you with praise for him?

Unwind and Relax

That's where he restores and revives my life.
He opens before me the right path
and leads me along in his footsteps of righteousness
so that I can bring honor to his name.

Psalm 23:3 tpt

Behavioral therapy involves a technique which teaches people to tense their bodies and then relax them. Repeating this exercise helps identify when our bodies are stressed and what to do to ease that tension. This process of relaxing the body when combined with proper breathing exercises releases hormones that increase tranquility and reduce anxiety.

While this is helpful with behavioral issues, the technique isn't just for those who seek therapy. We all need to learn how to unwind and relax our minds and bodies. This helps our creativity at work and home by engaging the part of our minds that is dormant when we are focused or stressed. Cortisol is released as stress levels increase. Relaxing maintains healthy levels of this hormone which affects every cell in the body. A feeling of serenity and calmness also opens our hearts and minds so we can effectively read the Word and listen to the Holy Spirit.

What do you do to relax your mind and body before meditating on God's Word?

REFINEMENT

The words of the LORD are flawless,
like silver purified in a crucible,
like gold refined seven times.

PSALM 12:6 NIV

The refinement of oil, sugar, metals, and other products is a process that humans have learned to do to improve the quality and longevity of an element. When these elements are refined by heat, it removes the impurities, so we have a product that remains pure for a longer time. The unwanted elements are removed, and we have something we can use for good purposes.

Not unlike these basic elements, God means for us to be refined. As we are all aware, we are far from pure. Even when we behave, say for a day or two, we are still far from holy. God intends to present to Jesus a pure and spotless church. He allows us to be refined and to be tested with the purpose of moving us closer to purity. He pushes us into full faith mode, so we have nothing left to give but our entire lives, and we recognize our desperate need for him.

What or who is Jesus using at work to refine you? Can you see the situation as an opportunity for your own growth?

HOLY GROUND

Since the creation of the world God's invisible qualities—his eternal power and divine nature—have been clearly seen, being understood from what has been made, so that people are without excuse.

ROMANS 1:20 NIV

One day we will understand what holy ground is. We will bow down in reverence before a holy God. We read in the Bible the stories of how a man died touching the ark of the covenant, and how Moses looked at the back of God as he passed by yet glowed with God's reflected glory. Elijah called down rain and fire that desecrated the false prophets. God's awesome power was displayed in such magnificent ways that people fell down in veneration or even death.

We worship God for this holy power, but also because of his mercy and grace. We follow him because of his patience, love, and kindness. And while his mercy flows, we have the opportunity to share with those who do not know him. While mercy is abundant in this time, we need to let others know about him. One day his holiness, power, justice, and mercy, will come together and we will all fully comprehend and revere the holy God.

What can you do to encourage others to revere God?

KEEP DIGGING

Bear one another's burdens,
and thereby fulfill the law of Christ.

GALATIANS 6:2 NASB

When we share our problems with another person, it is sometimes amazing the different perspective they can provide. But wisdom comes to those who seek it. It's worthwhile to seek the right person to confide in in order to find wisdom. It's like digging a hole to make a well. You dig until the water bubbles up, but to get to that point you have to actually start doing the digging, and you have to stick with it for a very long time to get to the water. That is what good teammates do; they stick with each other through the process of resolution until the issue is resolved.

In our roles as leaders we need people we can rely on to share our burdens. When God made Adam, he said it is not good for man to be alone. You were not made to walk through your troubles isolated from the help you can get from others. A full understanding of your burdens and how to resolve them comes from being able to share the perspective as well as the workload. Start digging with good counsel and stick with it until new insight bubbles up.

Who can you talk through life's problems with?

WITHOUT ARROGANCE

"Do not keep talking so proudly
or let your mouth speak such arrogance,
for the LORD is a God who knows,
and by him deeds are weighed."

1 SAMUEL 2:3 NIV

We can hear those blustery, arrogant people across the restaurant, on the street, or in the airport. They talk loudly about their own achievements and how well they have done for themselves. Their boasting drips with pride, and their attempts to lure gullible people into believing their stories is quite nauseating. The Lord is watching. He hears them. Our reactions to the bluster and bragging pale in comparison to the anger the Lord has. He will deal swiftly and justly with those who walk in pride and especially those who lead the weak astray.

Our role is to promote peace and extend an alternative voice to the despairing ones who need to hear truth without any arrogance. We must also guard against our own pride. We have accomplished good things and we can lead people. That can allow us to be pleased with ourselves and our achievements. That alone in not necessarily a sin, but when we do not acknowledge the one who gave us the positions and the skills, it can all be removed as quickly as it began.

What keeps you from becoming proud?

SPECIAL SKILLS

The LORD has given them special skills as engravers,
designers, embroiderers in blue, purple, and scarlet thread
on fine linen cloth, and weavers. They excel as craftsmen
and as designers.

EXODUS 35:35 NLT

If you have been to an art museum and have read and
learned about the artists, you will find that they have
surprisingly creative messages represented in their static
pictures. Creativity shows up in many forms in our lives
from great music to meaningful writing. But nothing is more
creative than the people and the creatures whom God made
and the world he created for us live in. Take time to watch
a show on the unique animals in creation. It is astounding
what they can do. God is the King of all creation.

Boredom and vulnerability can be incredible activators
for our greatest moments of creativity. Why? We need
time, and we need emotion. Those songs, books, paintings,
and movies that move us often bear the markings of a
bared soul. People who open up and share what they have
experienced create beauty for the world to ponder.

What would you create if no one were looking?

WHATEVER AGE

"Watch yourselves lest your hearts be weighed down with dissipation and drunkenness and cares of this life, and that day come upon you suddenly like a trap. For it will come upon all who dwell on the face of the whole earth. But stay awake at all times, praying that you may have strength to escape all these things that are going to take place, and to stand before the Son of Man."

LUKE 21:34-36 ESV

When we think about how much longer the average lifespan is now compared to a few hundred years ago, we have a lot more years to accrue wealth and to also dissipate it. Before the 1800s, people the world over could expect to live into their thirties but not normally a lot longer. Forties would have been quite an accomplishment! But in the modern world we consider the seventies too young to leave this earth.

Whether it is thirty years or ninety years, why waste any life with heavy hearts and overindulgences? Let's be a generous, thankful people and prepare ourselves for Christ's return. Let's pray for mercy and salvation for all. Let's pray that God will keep us from the wrath that is going to come upon the earth.

What do you notice about the times and seasons you are experiencing now?

PATTERN OF PERSISTENCE

The plans of the diligent lead to profit
as surely as haste leads to poverty.

PROVERBS 21:5 NIV

Diligence is rewarded; persistence breaks down barriers.
Pillars of rock in a cave are created by consistently dripping
water which deposits minerals to form stalactites and
stalagmites. Nature demonstrates that over time and despite
strong resistance, stubborn determination typically wins.
Consistent, unrelenting actions yield results.

Despite a great deal of resistance, expressed hatred, and
incredible suffering, Christ was determined to complete
his mission. He died willingly and with great suffering for
us. May we have the same fortitude in doing the will of
God. Perhaps there are small adjustments that need to be
made when facing tribulations, but ultimately a pattern
of steadfast behavior will be rewarded. Leaders are in a
unique position to help the members of their teams to be
purposefully industrious in a similar manner.

*What keeps you persisting in a task? How can you get your
team to the same place mentally and spiritually?*

REASONABLE PEOPLE

The wisdom from above is first pure, then peaceable, gentle, open to reason, full of mercy and good fruits, impartial and sincere.

JAMES 3:17 ESV

Reasonable people can use their sound thinking to understand how to follow a process or a set of instructions. Their emotional state is balanced, and they are attuned to what is expected of them and what others are expressing. Have you tried to talk with someone who is unraveling? Their emotions have overtaken their response systems; their thoughts cannot process in their prefrontal cortex. They respond with illogical and unrealistic answers often mixed with over-expressive emotions.

We have witnessed these people from various countries, genders, and ages. Is there any sense in trying to talk to them or even trying to help them? Yes, however it takes a reasonable and patient person. We can help them just as Jesus did, and we should consider it part of our ministry to do so. Someday we could be that person who needs patient help in order to level our thoughts.

Of all the people you know, who has helped exemplify patience and care for others? How?

GIVE TO CAESAR

Jesus said, "give to Caesar what belongs to Caesar,
and give to God what belongs to God."
His reply completely amazed them.

MARK 12:17 NLT

Partnerships, S Corps, extensions, quarterly taxes, yearly taxes—some time this year we pay taxes, and some of us will pay multiple times. It is the right of the government to collect on services rendered to the citizens of a country. The few who are exempt live without the burden of taxes. It can be an ethical dilemma for every person when they see how much the government takes. It has been the case for all of history.

Jesus was challenged a few times regarding taxes, and he gave such a simple answer. Render what is due to the government or kingdom in charge. Give to God what is due to him. In the same chapter, he told the story of the widow who gave all she had to God. Whether we are giving to the government or to God, we should question if something is right or wrong , but when we question it for our own gain, we need to lean into the counsel found in Scripture. God wants us to trust in him, not in how we can cheat the government out of taxes. Render it. Trust God.

When it comes to money, do you trust God to take care of you?

Good Timing

Everyone enjoys giving great advice.
But how delightful it is to say the right thing
at the right time!

PROVERBS 15:23 TPT

It is said that good timing is everything. If you play sports, you know timing is critical to making a successful play. Whether you are passing the ball to a receiver or swinging the bat at a pitch, the appropriate timing results in a positive play. Delaying in a race puts you in a tough spot to win. If you play an instrument and your timing is off, the performance is disrupted. Being late to work is not fitting and can result in punitive action. Similarly, our words must be appropriate. It is not good to make a joke at a funeral or share your darkest emotions at someone's celebration. But the right word at the right time is like a cool drink on a hot day.

We know what is appropriate by what we have learned. Society most often dictates what is and is not appropriate. However, for those who follow Christ, his Word and the Holy Spirit are our adjudicators. Scripture says that in the last days what is evil will be called good and what is good will be called evil. We must establish then what is appropriate through our relationship with God.

How have you established God's Word as your guide to what is appropriate?

ALWAYS THERE

A friend is always loyal,
and a brother is born to help in time of need.

PROVERBS 17:17 NLT

We all have that friend who is there when we need help, just to hang out with, or to listen to us when we need to complain. Even those with few friends have that one reliable person. For some, it just might even be our dog—man's best friend is incredibly dependable. If we go away, or if we are angry at our friend, or if we just can't be bothered with the relationship, our dog's loyalty can provide stability. Whomever, or whatever, it is these loyal ones who help us find something steady in a world that experiences constant change.

When we live for Christ and follow him, we have a steady friend in the Holy Spirit. He was sent to be our comforter and our counselor. He is our truthful, loyal, come-back-to-us companion. Realistically, we come back to him when we repent because he never actually left us to begin with. Perhaps that is what dogs do, too—they just wait for us to come around.

In what ways do you exemplify dependability to those you lead?

Do Not Forget

Be careful, and watch yourselves closely so that you do not forget the things your eyes have seen or let them fade from your heart as long as you live. Teach them to your children and to their children after them.

DEUTERONOMY 4:9 NIV

God encouraged the Israelites to remember his miracles and his great works. He wanted them to know that he was a God of the miraculous. He knew that when they were settled in their land and became fat on its goodness, they would forget how they got there. So, he said that they needed to be watchful and to make sure their memory of his works did not fade. Each generation was to be capable of speaking about their astounding God who could do the miraculous when needed.

We are the same because we also need constant reminders of God's goodness and his amazing power. We also can be distracted by this mundane life. Our faith can diminish because we are not careful to remember what he has done. Let faith arise! Let our hearts be encouraged by his wondrous deeds and his mighty hand.

What miracles have you witnessed or heard about which you can tell others?

ACTIVE PARTICIPANT

The word of God is living and active, and sharper than any two-edged sword, even penetrating as far as the division of soul and spirit, of both joints and marrow, and able to judge the thoughts and intentions of the heart.

HEBREWS 4:12 NASB

Activity infers that something is alive—the ant scurries around preparing for winter and the lion prowls at night for prey. However, when it comes to words that we read on paper, how can they be active? The answer is found in the source of the words themselves. It is the source of the words that actively makes the Word of God alive.

Jesus is the Word of God, and the Holy Spirit is the active participant. This is why the Word is able to judge the intentions of the heart because God is the source. This concept is explained in the gospels when Jesus encountered the centurion. The centurion believed that Jesus could simply speak, and his Word would be carried out. The centurion believed this because he understood authority. There is no greater authority than the one who spoke the sun, moon, and stars into existence. Today, in your life, Jesus' Word is active. Take time to listen for it.

What is Jesus actively speaking to you about today?

NOT AN EEYORE

Let the message of Christ dwell among you richly as you teach and admonish one another with all wisdom through Psalms, hymns, and songs from the Spirit, singing to God with gratitude in your hearts.

COLOSSIANS 3:16 NIV

Do you know someone who is a whistler? Perhaps you hear someone humming as they work. Likely that person is a merry old soul. They are happy to be alive and pleased to be doing whatever they put their hand to. There is no rain cloud following them around. They are not the *Eeyores* of the workplace. This kind of positivity is not flippant though; there is a deep joy that comes from a perspective which allows happiness to bubble over. The individual may not always be bubbly, but they likely reflect an overall optimism consistency in their lives.

As we learn to be thankful in all circumstances, to appreciate what we have, and to love beyond ourselves, we can take ahold of this cheerful demeanor. Much of it comes from an attitude of gratitude.

What can you be thankful for throughout the day today?

DRIVEN TO DO

Their purpose is to teach people to live disciplined and successful lives, to help them do what is right, just, and fair.

PROVERBS 1:3 NLT

It is an inherent part of being human that we want to be known. We do not want to be truly alone where no one understands or loves us for who we are. But once that is secured, we long for something to do. We have never been able to sit idle. Even those who have nothing to do end up doing something. As a side note, this is encouraging to us as managers because we are helping people live disciplined and successful lives. Every person has the same two deep needs: being known and having a purpose.

God knows you, but do you know your own purpose? That is a lifelong quest because it often changes during different seasons. Reflect on your life. Over the sands of time, did your drive to do something shift? At the core, everyone's purpose is to seek God. When you do that, he reveals what it is he wants you to do, and that brings satisfaction. In this pursuit you will gratify both needs: being known and knowing your purpose.

Despite your daily role in life, what do you think you were made for?

COMMANDING RESPECT

Show yourself in all respects to be a model of good works,
and in your teaching show integrity, dignity, and sound
speech that cannot be condemned, so that an opponent
may be put to shame, having nothing evil to say about us.

TITUS 2:7-8 ESV

There are people in our lives who command respect.
They are mostly seasoned with salt-and-pepper hair, and
perhaps they are a bit overly salted, but in a good way.
They are calm, respectful, and patient. They demonstrate
an uncommon level of consideration for others. Even
when they have strong opinions on matters, they wait to
express them; if they don't have the opportunity, they would
rather listen anyway. It provokes greater thought within
themselves.

They ponder the life of the young person they used to
be and how much they have learned since that time.
Their actions are intentionally self-sacrificing, and this
strengthens others even at their own expense. The objective
in their lives is to finish well by serving others so those they
serve have the confidence and ability to pass the same on to
the next generation.

*What do you do to inspire respect in the next generation of
leaders?*

Invisible Qualities

Ever since the world was created, people have seen the earth and sky. Through everything God made, they can clearly see his invisible qualities—his eternal power and divine nature. So they have no excuse for not knowing God.

ROMANS 1:20 NLT

An engineer was hired by a company to find the solution to a problem that others could not resolve. He visited the client, listened to the issue, considered what was wrong, and provided an elegant solution. It was a brief visit, but the company was up and running quickly. The owners were very pleased. Later in the month, they received a large bill beyond what they considered reasonable. They spoke to the engineer, and he responded that it was not about time but about his sophisticated, well-designed repair. It was about knowing what to do, not how long it took. They could not deny his brilliance and paid the bill.

Like the example in the story, elegance comes in many forms. When people ponder creation and see its sophistication and God's redemptive plan, they cannot excuse their ignorance. They deny him because they don't want to pay the cost due to the engineer behind it all.

When you look around, what stands out as elegant?

Quiet Moments

I am standing in absolute stillness,
silent before the one I love,
waiting as long as it takes for him to rescue me.
Only God is my Savior, and he will not fail me.

PSALM 62:5 TPT

Have you ever been by the water alone and the waves are gently lapping on the shore? Or have you been in the woods when a light breeze is blowing but there is not a sound otherwise? Have you stood on a mountaintop and gazed out over the valley, and no one else is in sight? These are places of real stillness and quiet. It's so silent that you can hear the sound of leaves rustling in a light breeze or water rippling in a brook.

Sometimes you can find these moments of quiet in a cabin by the lake or in a park late at night. We rarely find them in our electronically stimulated homes which always seem to be abuzz. Conversely, these places are so still you can hear your own breathing and the beating of your heart. God loves to be in those still, quiet places with you.

Where do you find quiet moments to meet with God?

THE OLD MONK

I pray that the eyes of your heart may be enlightened, so
that you will know what is the hope of His calling, what are
the riches of the glory of His inheritance in the saints.

EPHESIANS 1:18 NASB

Two Chinese monks were meditating. The younger monk
asked the older one, "What do you see in me?" The older
monk said he saw a stately buddha. The young monk was
pleased. After a while, the older monk asked the younger
monk the same question. Thinking he was sly, the younger
monk replied that he saw a pile of dung. The old man
smiled but did not respond. When the day was over, the
young monk went home, and he proudly relayed the story
to his sister. He thought he had outwitted the old monk.
She laughed at him and explained that he had not outwitted
anyone. "What you see is what you are, not what he is. That
means your heart is a pile of dung."

Jesus talked about how important our hearts are: from
the outflow of our hearts our mouths will speak. Paul
encouraged us to allow our hearts to see God, so we
become like him.

*When you think about others and talk about them, what do
you see reflected in these thoughts and words about yourself?*

ACCOUNTABILITY MATTERS

Confess yours sins to each other and pray for each other
so that you may be healed.

JAMES 5:16 NIV

As leaders we feel the pressure to be strong, brave, and
tenacious in the face of trouble. There is an innate sense
that this is what is needed to be in charge. So when it comes
to confessing our weaknesses to one another, we have a
very difficult time. It creates trouble in our hearts. Much
of this conundrum lies in our own perception of who we
should be and how we prove that to be true. Or in most
cases, how we are not performing the way we think we
should. We have the external pressure to portray strength,
and an unmet internal standard that shames us into silence.
It is hard to answer for any area of failure whether at work,
home, or within ourselves.

What is amazing and relieving is God's grace for us in our
many failures. He holds the measurement and the final
accounting. He has mercy on us, and his grace empowers
us to choose to live for him. We can turn to others and find
relief in confession and healing prayer for our weary souls.

*Do you have someone you can be vulnerable with, and
confess your weaknesses and failings to?*

September

Do nothing from selfish ambition or conceit,
but in humility count others more significant
than yourselves.

PHILIPPIANS 2:3 ESV

No Longer Orphans

You Gentiles are no longer strangers and foreigners.
You are citizens along with all of God's holy people.
You are members of God's family.

EPHESIANS 2:19 NLT

Family relationships can be traumatic at times; they are not always happy. So when we read a verse like today's, our responses can be guarded because we have been hurt by our families or even by God's own people. But the focus of this text is for those who had no place with God. If we put ourselves in that position, which is hard to truly imagine, we would be incredibly grateful to be a part of his people.

Consider the orphan who has no home. Would they want to be part of the same family who hurt you? Yes, desperately so. At least they would belong somewhere instead of nowhere. In fact, this thinking can bring us helpful healing and forgiveness as we dwell upon what it means to have no family at all. It doesn't right any wrongs, but it does give us a healthy perspective. How great it is that we are now grafted into God's family! No one ever needs to feel alone. We all belong to him.

How can you care for orphans today?

Be Yourself

I praise you, for I am fearfully and wonderfully made.
Wonderful are your works;
my soul knows it very well.

PSALM 139:14 ESV

Father and son were walking along the beach and skipping stones together across the smooth water. They tossed some driftwood into the ocean and started bombing it. They threw big stones and little stones as they tried to perfect the drop so a stone would land right on top of the wood. The son was impressed by his father's accuracy. He looked up at his father with admiration thinking he was the best in the world at rock throwing. There is probably someone in the world more practiced than we are at certain things, but we can be the best at being ourselves.

Authenticity is the honest evaluation which develops into an unadulterated understanding of ourselves. We can be genuine about who we are. Our confidence is in our Creator and who he made us to be, not in acquiring the title of "best" at anything other than being ourselves.

Where does your personal value come from?

Juicy Morsel

One who conceals an offense seeks love,
But one who repeats a matter separates close friends.

PROVERBS 17:9 NASB

Cutting into a nicely cooked steak gets those salivary glands pumping. We happily anticipate the enticing smell, the taste of salt and spices, and the deep, rich flavor of the meat. Mmm. Delicious. So also, is the juicy morsel of gossip anticipated and savored: that secret knowledge of another person, whether friend or foe, feeds the temptation. Gossip doesn't care. Its goal is to destroy the sinner. But love conceals a matter. It does not boast of knowledge. It covers the repentant.

Imagine all those dark thoughts which you deeply conceal being exposed for all to see. What if your respected mentor knew of all your hidden secrets? What shame and hurt that would cause. It's horrifying to think of facing others' judgment. But Jesus is discreet. His love covers our sins, and he does not expose us even when he could. Our sins are against him, yet he shelters us. Let's be a place of safety and discretion for the people in our lives, not with the objective of encouraging sin but rather to allow for people to heal and grow.

What can you do to discourage gossip and encourage grace?

KEY TO UNDERSTANDING

If you are wise and understand God's ways, prove it
by living an honorable life, doing good works with the
humility that comes from wisdom.

JAMES 3:13 NLT

Do you lack understanding? Seek wisdom. Do you lack
compassion? Seek understanding. Understanding requires
a person to have a combination of both knowledge and
awareness. It encompasses our thoughts and our emotions
and merges them together into action. When actively
working, understanding is observable in an honorable life
which is full of good works and carried out with humility.
Much of what we do to lead others must incorporate this
attention to being an understanding person; it comes by
acquiring the wisdom and knowledge of God.

The key to this wisdom and knowledge is found in the
person of the Holy Spirit. He has been sent to us to bring
truth, and to teach, counsel, and comfort us. He is the
Spirit of understanding, and within his presence is both
the knowledge and emotive action that demonstrates
understanding.

*When you are trying to understand a situation, do you seek
the Holy Spirit's activity and hear his voice?*

To Be Truly Known

Now we see only a reflection as in a mirror;
then we shall see face to face. Now I know in part;
then I shall know fully, even as I am fully known.

1 CORINTHIANS 13:12 NIV

If there is one desire common to mankind which drives much of what we do, it is to be known, truly known, and accepted. How many of us acknowledge this in our day-to-day movements? Our common focus as leaders is to achieve success, build wealth, find security, receive accolades, and grow our empire. The bigger and greater that empire is, the better we are. Even if we don't find success in these things, we still desire them and believe they will validate us.

We also want relationships, but those are often treated as secondary to those other goals. However, we will find joy and contentment when we realize and accept that our validation comes from being known as we are without a string of achievements. Jesus encourages us to be known by him, and to confidently come before the Father to whom we belong.

How can you take time to allow God to see you?

BEING AUTHORITATIVE

That power is the same as the mighty strength he exerted
when he raised Christ from the dead and seated him at
his right hand in the heavenly realms, far above all rule
and authority, power and dominion, and every name that
is invoked, not only in the present age but also in
the one to come.

EPHESIANS 1:19-21 NIV

Not to be confused with *authoritarian* which has a negative
connotation, *authoritative* has a positive meaning. It means
to be trusted, confident, and commanding. An authoritative
person knows what they are talking about and is reliable
in what they say. It is like the captain who sailed for forty
years talking to a new ship hand about the dangers of the
ocean. It's the rookie quarterback listening to the GOAT
(greatest of all time) share about what he wished he knew
when he started. It is about a man who has owned multiple
companies sharing with new businessmen the importance
of having vision and purposeful planning.

The finest example of being authoritative is seen in Jesus
Christ. He is the ultimate authority. He knows all things
and is able to do all things.

*What can you share with others to help them as future
leaders?*

SEASONED TRUTH

The king is pleased with words from righteous lips;
he loves those who speak honestly.

PROVERBS 16:13 NLT

When you think of someone who is honest, what qualities
come to mind? Do you think of someone who is authentic,
true, and real? Is there anything better than a friend or a
co-worker who is honest? This is not referring to a person
who is brash and blurts out their every thought; it means
the one who understands themselves and is able to speak
the truth seasoned with this knowledge. That person is
not only trustworthy, but they offer a breath of fresh air to
whomever they work with.

Jesus demonstrated the completeness of an honest person.
He seasoned his truth with love and understood himself in
the context of his circumstances. His identity was hidden
within his relationship with the Father, so he was sure of
himself and did not need the approval of man. When he
spoke, it wasn't for manipulative purposes. Those who were
with him could completely trust his motives. Jesus allows us
to be vulnerable with him because we can trust him at his
word. That's also what honesty can do for those you lead.

How does honesty show up in your life?

CONSIDERING OTHERS

Let us consider how to stir up one another
to love and good works.

HEBREWS 10:24 ESV

When you encounter a rude person, what is your first response? We often don't respond well or in a civil manner. It takes a disciplined person to answer well to insolence. God desires that we learn how to control our responses and to be gallant even when we are not receiving similar courtesy.

How refreshing it is when we meet someone who is well-mannered and considerate. Those people are a delight to be with. They speak with gentleness which gives rise to good conversations. In order to be courteous, we need to learn how to lay aside our preferences and to first serve others. This can be something our parents instilled in us early in life, or we can learn it now. It is never too late to start considering others! A simple beginning could be as small as opening doors for your team members as you have the opportunity.

What can you do to improve your consideration of others?

MAKING IT WORK

Lazy people want much but get little,
but those who work hard will prosper.

PROVERBS 13:4 NLT

The determined businessman was going to make things
work. He worked day after day, stubbornly persevering.
His life was in God's hands, and he knew it. He also knew
that God had given him the gift of tenacity, so he did not
stop. Building a business takes a kind of dogged attitude.
Slowly but surely, he saw results as one customer spoke
to another, and his client base grew. Word got out about
his unwavering commitment and that he was service-
oriented and purposeful in his work. Within a few years,
he branched out into other services. Sole proprietors
came to him, and not having the same determination they
subjugated themselves to become part of his company.
Within a few years, his resolute and driven work ethic
resulted in a multimillion-dollar corporation that provided
multiple services to thousands of customers.

God didn't create us to be idle. Being so leads us into dark
places because our drive pushes us somewhere. We are
never idle; we just end up sinning. If we have nothing to
do but entertain ourselves, we must change. We must be
staunch in maintaining an active pursuit of God and service
to others.

As a new season begins, what can you purposefully pursue?

BEST CARETAKER

*We should love people not only with words and talk,
but by our actions and true caring.*

1 JOHN 3:18 NCV

If you were to enter the hospital as a patient today, what
sort of caretaker would you want to look after you? If you
were at home and unable to take care of yourself, who
would you want by your side? According to research,
people want caregivers that comfort, confirm, and build
a relationship. People want friends with them when they
are suffering. They also want to know that they matter and
that they are important. A lot of people want their mothers
when they are hurting.

When we consider the ideal attributes of mothers and
friends, these words come to mind: kind, thoughtful,
considerate, loving, gentle, sensitive, and attentive. This
defines a caring. Christ was a caring man. He loved
those around him, helped anyone in need, healed many,
and grieved with those who were grieving. He was an
example of a truly caring friend and leader.

*How can you demonstrate caring like Christ did to those you
encounter?*

STANDING TOGETHER

When troubles of any kind come your way, consider it an opportunity for great joy. For you know that when your faith is tested, your endurance has a chance to grow.

JAMES 1:2-3 NLT

Jesus said that a city that is divided will be ruined and house that is divided will fall, but he made it abundantly clear that those who build their house upon God's Word will stand. We can have squabbles at work, but when competition threatens to close our doors, workers unite to overcome the adversary.

Not dissimilar to this sense of camaraderie and protection is when we witness our communities and countries also standing together against foreign attacks. We can have internal disruptions, but when external forces come against us, stout unity can quickly form. History has taught us that families, communities, and countries are resilient when it comes to resisting an enemy, and the more unified they are, the more durability they demonstrate. In our faith, family, and communities, our time together encourages the unity which we need to endure. We must remain together until Jesus returns and heals our brokenness and brings us peace.

How can you encourage unity and strength amongst those around you?

COMPREHENSIVE SALVATION

God is able to make every grace overflow to you,
so that in every way, always having everything you need,
you may excel in every good work.

2 CORINTHIANS 9:8 CSB

If someone did not know anything about God but read the
Bible and studied all that God did, and then they contrast it
with how Christians live, would they wonder if God had really
saved us? Is he really enough? What is lacking in us that we
are not able to fully embrace his abundant love and life?

God's salvation is comprehensive. It is not limited liability
coverage. Jesus paid for our insurance in full. Not only did
he provide insurance but also the means to live abundantly.
The issue is not his provision; it is our dependence.
Do we live like we need him? Most of us live without
any desperation for the love of God. Who wants to be
desperate? There are times when we need him, and he is
faithfully there for us. But God wants us to get to that place
of needing him desperately every moment of every day. We
agree, Jesus! Help us get there!

How can you learn to depend on God daily?

RESPONSIBLE FOR MUCH

"Whoever can be trusted with very little can also be trusted with much, and whoever is dishonest with very little will also be dishonest with much."

LUKE 16:10 NIV

The more responsibilities we have, the weightier life becomes… if we take those obligations seriously. We need Jesus to help us. Those who are not conscientious about what they accomplished often find themselves with little responsibility in the end. That is the point of today's Scripture. Even though Christ's emphasis is on money, this principle applies to how we manage anything in life. If we can be trusted with a little, we can be trusted with more. This is how we ended up leading a team of people.

How we manage small things plays out in how we manage larger ones. We can see this principle at work with possessions, emotions, and even spiritual responsibilities. Let us carefully guard the responsibilities and gifts we have been given and use them to glorify God.

Whom do you trust in leadership and why do you trust them specifically? Why does God trust you to lead?

LIVE FREELY

Without faith living within us it would be impossible to
please God. For we come to God in faith knowing that
he is real and that he rewards the faith of those
who passionately seek him.

HEBREWS 11:6 TPT

God sent Jesus to earth in order for him to suffer and die in
our place. Jesus paid the ultimate price for us. He humbled
himself and put aside his heavenly position. He was born a
baby, grew to be a man, was horrifically beaten and put to
death as an innocent person. It was the will of God that he
be punished for our misdeeds. It was the will of God that he
died for our sins. His death gave us life.

This is what we believe, and this is what enables us to live
freely before God and not under his wrath. Our belief in
this truth, and our faith in Jesus Christ and his precious
sacrifice is what pleases our Father. We rejoice that we
are saved, and we are happy that our salvation has been
accomplished. Now we wait expectantly for his return
and our resurrection. We know that this life is temporary,
and we anticipate with expectant hearts the amazing
promises that no eye has seen, nor ear has heard. We will be
astounded at what he will reveal to us.

What makes you excited about your eternal existence?

Valued Administrator

Do you see a man skillful in his work?
He will stand before kings;
he will not stand before obscure men.

PROVERBS 22:29 ESV

As administrative types, the organizers see the most effective way of running a process, so it is completed efficiently and with excellence. They know how to lay out an idea, highlight all the barriers, and eliminate roadblocks with competency. Everything they do has a process so it can be adjusted and improved. That's efficiency!

Efficient people are recognized. They are valued for what they can accomplish. They are the top five percent of the twenty percent who do eighty percent of the work in the world. Effectiveness like this is both a gift as well as a quality that can be developed. As managers, when we find an effective and proficient person, we may feel like we have won the lottery. It is important then to value these special souls, make sure they have whatever they need to use their innate abilities, and allow them mental breaks so they stay fresh and rested!

How can you make sure your MVP of administration and detail is rested?

GRACE RETURNED

Your goodness is as high as the mountains.
Your justice is as deep as the great ocean.
LORD, you protect both people and animals.

PSALM 36:6 NCV

Who doesn't love a good movie that shows justice being served in the end? We dislike it when the bad guy gets away with anything. This theme has been prevalent in humanity since the beginning of time. We long for things to be made right, especially where we are personally involved.

Oddly enough, if we are the perpetrator, we want to be shown grace when we are caught. We like the idea of getting away with the naughty deed. What wicked people we are! Whether it is in our workplaces, our homes, or society in general, we want justice; however, personally, we want to avoid punishment. At the very least, we want mercy for the things we do to harm others. Thank God that he is a gracious and righteous judge. Jesus said that we will be judged by the very manner in which we judge others. Let us show grace to one another so we also will be treated with grace.

How do you judge those around you, and consequently, how do you think you should be judged?

FULLY COMMITTED

Commit to the LORD whatever you do,
and he will establish your plans.

PROVERBS 16:3 NIV

The wind ferociously whipped at the parachuter's face. At around 120 miles per hour, it just about blew his helmet off when he first stepped up to the side opening of the plane. He contemplated all the concerns he had thought about earlier—the what-ifs of life. It was too late now. He was committed. Actually, he was beyond committed; it was happening. As soon as he reached the doorway, the wind sucked him out. It was an odd sensation, like being tossed by a wave in the ocean. It was both violent and peaceful. Seconds passed. He started to feel himself go into free-fall when a sharp jerk suddenly startled him, and the parachute fluttered open. Thank God. Now to navigate the landing.

It takes a serious level of unswerving resolve to jump out of a plane and then trust a piece of cloth to deliver a safe landing. Commitment to God and his purposes should look like that to us. We are fully in his hands, and we trust him to land us securely. Let's grit our teeth and dive deeply into what God has planned for us!

How have you seen God establish the pursuits which you have given to him?

DIRECT PRAISE

Praise the LORD!
Praise God in his sanctuary;
praise him in his mighty heaven!
Praise him for his mighty works;
praise his unequaled greatness.

PSALM 150:1-2 NLT

When you encounter a person you admire, perhaps a business owner, an athlete, or an artist, how easy is it to say something good about them? Most of us wouldn't find it hard to praise them. Throngs of admirers often surround famous people. You may not even get close enough to say anything if you wanted to try. Our motivations are usually selfish in these situations. We usually want to engage an accomplished person for our own gratification, so we can say we spoke with them, or we can boast about something we've done.

God, who is more famous, talented, and admirable than anyone ever, receives our praise directly. He also responds personally, and he wants us to boast all about how we know him. That's what it means to praise God. He wants us to tell everyone about who we know and what he has done. Praise him!

How does your praise for God look to others?

THE CATTLE PROD

Do not be children in your thinking.
Be infants in evil, but in your thinking be mature.

1 CORINTHIANS 14:20 ESV

Sanctification is critical in the life of the believer. We are saved by grace and not by our works, but it does not stop there. The sanctifying work of the Spirit continues in our lives to spur us on in growing to be more like Christ. It is too easy to rest on the laurels of salvation, so the Spirit pokes at us like a farmer does with a cattle prod to his livestock. The Spirit moves us along, so we don't become stagnant in our faith.

God allows for us to face tests and trials for the purpose of growing a dependency on his Spirit. He doesn't want us to boast in our flesh but to boast about him as he works in us to bring about maturity. It is important for us to notice his work, and it is encouraging to see how we have grown over the years. Examining our refinement is necessary. We should take time to review what has changed in our habits, person, and spiritual connection with God. Our goal is to love him wholeheartedly and out of this, we learn how to love and serve others.

In what ways have you matured so far this year?

PEACEFUL STATE

May the Lord of peace himself give you peace
at all times in every way. The Lord be with you all.

2 THESSALONIANS 3:16 ESV

The most serene people are those who have left this life in peace. It is not scary to look at a family member in that peaceful state of death because you know where their spirit is, and they are better for it. For those of us left behind, we face the difficulty of maintaining our sense of tranquility in a world of chaos and sadness. Our only source of true peace is found in the rest we receive when we connect with God and wait upon him. He is our source of quietude—the calm in the storm.

The Holy Spirit comes to us in our most difficult seasons and offers serenity much like Jesus went to the disciples and calmed the storm. If we sit and meditate upon his Word, we will find hope and rest in the promises of our eternal home. There will not be rest in this life until he comes, but we can find serenity in our hearts before that.

*If a storm is raging around you, will you take time to sit
before the throne of God and ask for his peace?*

GROWING IN ENTHUSIASM

Work with enthusiasm, as though you were working
for the Lord rather than for people.

EPHESIANS 6:7 NLT

Peter was a man with enthusiasm. He was quick to speak,
swift to act, and full of passion. Sometimes it caused
trouble; Peter's zeal was for Jesus to take the throne and
become the King of Israel. He wanted to be a part of the
coup. He wanted to be a leader in that kingdom.

In his excitement, Peter didn't recognize God's timing.
But after Jesus death and resurrection, Peter's fervor grew
into an enduring faith filled with a wiser zeal. We read in
Acts that Jesus' words about Peter came true. Jesus built
the church using the well-known passion that Peter had
always shown. He took Peter's self-promoting enthusiasm
and turned it into an eagerness to preach the Word of God;
he led the early church in Jerusalem. Looking back on our
lives, do we see the younger, vivacious person we once were
becoming a seasoned leader?

*How can God capture your enthusiasm to lead for his
purposes?*

COURAGEOUS RESPONSE

"O man greatly loved, fear not, peace be with you;
be strong and of good courage." And as he spoke to me,
I was strengthened and said, "Let my lord speak,
for you have strengthened me."

DANIEL 10:19 ESV

Being courageous means facing one's fears and acting in opposition to what is instinctual. When one sees a disaster sweeping toward them, it is normal to flee. But how do the courageous respond when they see people threatened by the path of destruction? They do what is counterintuitive—they see the danger, face the fear, and embrace the potential loss. Courage is about accepting the possible loss, pain, or change, and forging ahead.

Leaders often face threatening situations and then take risks. It is a part of the mantle that has been placed upon us. We run to face the giant, not cower from it. But there is another courage that is deeper and more meaningful for those in close relationships with us; the courage to be vulnerable. In fact, the most courageous leader is the person who can accept themselves and live in this world without fear.

Today, can you shut out shame and allow others close to you to know more about who you are?

Demonstrated Ability

The things you have heard me say in the presence of many witnesses entrust to reliable people who will also be qualified to teach others.

2 Timothy 2:2 niv

The Bible makes it clear that there are requirements for those who want to teach the Word. To qualify you must have had good teaching, and you must have learned from it. You need to have the heart of a disciple. You must also be reliable. But these traits alone do not qualify you or necessarily demonstrate your competency.

Knowledge alone does not make someone competent. You must demonstrate ability as well as have had applicable experience and appropriate training. When a person is skilled enough, they may be deemed competent. This process is already instituted in many areas of learning today where you engage material in order to learn, but you still must fulfill a period of guided practice in order to become licensed. It is a thorough plan to equip someone in their preferred area of expertise. We require this level of experts in our workplaces regularly because they can function with reliability and excellence, especially as it relates to technical expertise.

You may know a lot about Christianity and the Word, but how do you practice it with the excellence required of a mature, knowledgeable leader?

CLEAR INSTRUCTIONS

One of them, an expert in the law, tested him with this question: "Teacher, which is the greatest commandment in the Law?" Jesus replied: "'Love the Lord your God with all your heart and with all your soul and with all your mind.' This is the first and greatest commandment. And the second is like it: 'Love your neighbor as yourself.' All the Law and the Prophets hang on these two commandments."

MATTHEW 22:35-39 NIV

It's time for a new desk; you get it ordered, and it's shipped. You excitedly sign for the receipt, but when you get it opened you realize it requires assembly. Uh-oh. Assembly instructions are often in another language, or in some form of illogical English, or there are pictures that don't make any sense. How frustrating when work is at a standstill because you can't understand the instructions to assemble your new workstation!

Thankfully, God made our instructions clear. It starts with *love God* and finishes with *love one another*. If we get that down, we are good to go. God's instructions are reasonable and wise—love God and love people. These are the greatest commandments and the clearest instructions. It is usually just our selfish ambitions that get in the way, but these are manageable by returning repeatedly to our sensible, beautiful instructions.

How can you teach, train, and love others better?

POSITIVE SENTIMENTS

When we get together, I want to encourage you in your faith, but I also want to be encouraged by yours.

ROMANS 1:12 NLT

Most of the time we don't need a lot of spoken words to push us in the right direction. A few positive sentiments that challenge our status quo can shake us out of apathy or pessimism pretty quickly. Encouragement is necessary in daily living, both in the receiving and in the giving. Exhortation may be necessary when we are really stuck in a rut. As we manage people, we hopefully never have to urge someone out of complacency. If we do, it is actually an honor to help a team member out of a funk. This is part of what we signed on for as a leader, and we want to make sure people know that we can take on a crisis or conflict with dexterity—at least most of the time!

The benefit of being a person who acts is that we get to see the results. We get to see our people be encouraged and increase their productivity. It's a blessing and an inspiration to us when we can be that positive voice in someone's life, and it encourages us so we can help the next team member when they need it.

What can you do to encourage someone today?

STRONGEST BRAID

Here's what I've learned through it all:
Don't give up; don't be impatient;
be entwined as one with the Lord.
Be brave and courageous, and never lose hope.
Yes, keep on waiting—for he will never disappoint you!

PSALM 27:14 TPT

When you are having problems finding material strong enough to tie items together or to hold a weight, you can bind strands of the same material together to greatly increase its strength. Braiding has been known and used for over four thousand years, and today we still use braided strands for ropes, cables, and protective coverings for plumbing.

Being entwined with the Lord gives us a strength that we would never have on our own. This close relationship with God allows us to be brave in the face of adversity and courageous in times of danger. Our inhibitions can be cast aside because we know well the faithful God we serve. His strands of wisdom will never break. As you have hope in the Lord to carry you through difficult seasons, be an anchor and an encouragement to those you serve. Show them what it looks like to be entwined with God.

How can you show your enduring hope to those you work with?

ALREADY CONFIRMED

This is no empty hope, for God himself is the one who has
prepared us for this wonderful destiny. And to confirm
this promise, he has given us the Holy Spirit, like an
engagement ring, as a guarantee.

2 CORINTHIANS 5:5 TPT

He felt the warm wash of shame. The embarrassment
of failure rushed over him. His face flushed red. His
boss stepped close and asked if he had confirmed the
reservation. This only made it worse for him. He looked
at the event coordinator with distress and pleaded to see if
there was anything that could be done.

Is there any worse feeling than shame? We can forget to
confirm something on a personal level and be frustrated
and angry at ourselves, but when we do it corporately;
that feels awful. We confirm things because we want to be
sure. Confirmation establishes and settles a matter. Our
salvation and promised resurrection are confirmed. It has
been completed in the person of Jesus Christ. We have this
assurance beyond just a wimpy hope. It is a fixed reality.

What about your future is certain and confirmed?

WHERE CREDIT IS DUE

"Whoever acknowledges me before others, I will also
acknowledge them before my Father in heaven."

MATTHEW 10:32 NIV

It is interesting to observe an award ceremony at work and
to take notice of all the back patting. A great teammate will
stand up and say he couldn't have done it without his team
or his leader. The leader will say his success was attributed
to the team. How many times do we see an employee stand
up and say, "That was all me; I made it happen"? Not often.
If someone did, they would likely be marginalized for their
arrogance by peers and leaders. A certain level of humility is
rightfully expected. Nobody is really that great on their own.

Jesus makes it clear that at the "end ceremony" he will know
who credited him and who took the glory for themselves.
We may think that this verse is oppressive in that it berates
us into not denying God. Rather, we should see it as
encouraging us to acknowledge our Father in the context of
our daily achievements. How much do we believe that our
successes are really attributed to us alone? Are we ready to
acknowledge the beautiful gifts showered on us by our good
and gracious God?

How can you give credit where credit is due?

COMFORTED TO COMFORT

Blessed be the God and Father of our Lord Jesus Christ, the Father of mercies and God of all comfort, who comforts us in all our affliction, so that we may be able to comfort those who are in any affliction, with the comfort with which we ourselves are comforted by God.

2 CORINTHIANS 1:3-4 ESV

We have been given a comforter in the person of the Holy Spirit. He was sent to us with the understanding and knowledge that humans are weak, needy, and struggling to overcome the brokenness of the world around them. He comforts those who are afflicted and suffering so they can heal and learn to comfort others.

We are all part of the plan to help those who are suffering. Perhaps we are currently at a place in our lives where we are strong, and we do not have the need for comfort. Then we are to comfort those in need. We are to use our positions and our influence to help others also turn to the Holy Spirit. Whether we are going through something ourselves, or we are actively comforting someone through a difficult time, Christ wants us healed and not isolated or left in pain. He came to break us free and to bring healing.

In what ways can you bring comfort to those who are in pain?

DISCIPLINE OF FASTING

Joyful are those you discipline, LORD,
those you teach with your instructions.

PSALM 94:12 NLT

Fasting. Just saying the word can make us quiver in our boots. The thought of not eating, drinking only water, or refraining from an activity we truly enjoy can feel like death. That is kind of the point. Fasting is a discipline that reminds us of our real needs in life and to alert us to our dependence on anything other than God. It also reminds us that we need to depend on God for all of life.

The regimen of regular fasting benefits us in teaching us self-control. This, in turn, invites God's favor and help. As we practice fasting, we learn to say no to comfort on a regular basis. We lean into our core need for more of God's Spirit. We also learn how to control our primal urges, and this has a direct correlation to gaining control over our impulses. For this reason fasting has a double health benefit: it improves our overall health, and it benefits our longevity. Perhaps us believers can add a third benefit as it improves our eternal health!

Are you maintaining discipline over your impulses?

OCTOBER

"Whoever would be great among you
must be your servant."

MATTHEW 20:26 ESV

STABLE IN CHOAS

Blessed be the God and Father of our Lord Jesus Christ,
who has blessed us in Christ with every spiritual blessing
in the heavenly places, even as he chose us in him before
the foundation of the world, that we should be holy and
blameless before him.

EPHESIANS 1:3-4 ESV

Our world is chaotic. Until Christ returns and establishes
his rule, it will continue to be so. We are not going to make
it better. In fact, the Bible makes it clear that it gets worse
before the end. This is why it is so important to find a stable
place. We may naturally look to our close relationships for
stability, or perhaps our job or our home. There are things
in life that are reasonably consistent and settled, but they
do not bring peace that is steady. We know our jobs can
be lost, and therefore so can our homes. Lives, God forbid,
can end abruptly and we can lose those we love. And
sometimes the pressures in life can create chaos in our close
relationships.

The presence of Christ and his Spirit with us is a consistent
and secure place for us to be established and stable.
We never have to feel overwhelmed by chaos with him
because our security is not in this world but in our eternal
relationship with Christ.

Why do you feel secure even when life around you is chaotic?

STRENGTH IN PAIN

I pray that from his glorious, unlimited resources he will
empower you with inner strength through his Spirit.

EPHESIANS 3:16 NLT

From the man's bearing you would not know that he
had only one arm. He carried himself with dignity and
power. His strength was obvious. When he set to a task, he
carried it out effectively and equal to that of his dual-fisted
compatriots. He could pick up a hundred pounds in one
arm and carry it without showing any strain. His family was
killed in the same incident in which he lost his arm, and the
scars on his heart were much deeper than those on his body.
Still, he remained steadfast in Christ, knowing that he would
see them again. His closeness to his Savior gave him the
strength and hope he needed each day to remain resilient in
the face of the worst pain, the loss of his loved ones.

When you face hard times, God has an unlimited ability
to comfort and strengthen you in more ways that you
understand. He pours out his Spirit on you so you will not
thirst or hunger for anything. His love is lavished on you
like you have never known possible. That is what makes you
strong. Trust in his empowering grace.

What do you need strength for today?

DRAWING EXCELLENCE

As iron sharpens iron,
so people can improve each other.

PROVERBS 27:17 NCV

You have the potential to inspire others as their leader. However, if you tell them that they need something more in their lives, their faith in you could cause them to think they don't have enough. You may even cause them to believe they are not enough as they are and in the way their Creator made them. That is society's message, commonly advertised as, *make your life better by adding this special something* or *your life is not enough without it*. We have even enriched our most basic nutrient—water! It seems that our culture has developed an enrichment complex. However, the reality is that we have become so full, and we have so much that we have become dull to the very good things God already made, like our people who are our greatest treasure.

When you see those whom you lead as the problem, or that they are not enough, they will not be part of any solution you desire. But as you resolve to find God's perspective and begin to see yourself as he sees you, you will understand the issues that are caused by people actually allow for growth and maturity in all. Through intentional sharpening and working with others, you can develop people who are getting and giving the best in life.

As you strive to draw excellence out of your team members, do you see how they are also calling you to a better standard?

TUG-OF-WAR

Make my joy complete by being of the same mind,
maintaining the same love, united in spirit,
intent on one purpose.

PHILIPPIANS 2:2 NASB

The game *tug-of-war* is about capturing and maintaining the balance of power. If you can get your opponent's team off balance, you can overpower them. When you are in a battle, you can pull as individuals, or you can pull in unity. When you are unified, it magnifies the strength of the individuals because the weight and force combine in one movement. It is often the breakthrough required to win.

Unity in our teammates at work and at church is not very different. When we are not individuated but instead combine our wills with a united purpose, we can accomplish greater things. It was Paul's intention to encourage us to unite because he knew that when we do, the Holy Spirit will come upon our people in greater measure and our combined power will be greatly increased. This means the world will see the power of God manifested in his people in far greater measure.

Unity may be easier to achieve in church because of a shared belief in God, but how can you encourage unity at work when people may not have the same spiritual beliefs?

SPONTANEOUS IN CONTEXT

If you live without restraint
and are unable to control your temper,
you're as helpless as a city with broken-down defenses,
open to attack.

PROVERBS 25:28 TPT

Have you ever been in public and suddenly done something socially unacceptable? If you stood up and started dancing and clapping at a restaurant, people would think you were strange. But put that same action at a rock concert and it is natural. Spontaneity is great in context, and sometimes good out of context. It is a natural response, unrestrained by social norms, and can bring life to a moment of tedium. Buy a random gift for someone for no reason. Dance in the rain.

A person cannot endlessly live a spontaneous life because it would undermine our human need for security and safety. People who have impulsive and unconstrained lives don't often end up in the best of places. We have balance for this reason. Allowing spontaneity to happen in a healthy manner is part of a good life, however, and it adds greatly to an enjoyable work environment.

What can you do spontaneously today for your team?

ADAPTATION CHALLENGE

When God's people are in need, be ready to help them.
Always be eager to practice hospitality.

ROMANS 12:13 NLT

One of our securities in life is to settle into a home and create a comfortable space that is safe from danger and protected from the elements. We need this as humans at a basic level to begin to explore deeper relationships and to develop healthy connections. But in this process of finding security we face the possibility of withdrawing and becoming stagnant or self-focused. Additionally, if our work roles become routine and predictable how are we challenged to grow and adapt?

When both our home and work environments limit our interactions with people, we should be aware and make a change. Of course, God has the answer, and it is found in a unique way. Inviting a stranger into our home is both vulnerable and opportunistic. The good news of Christ's redemption can be shared, and we are given the occasion to adapt to a new element in our lives. If we listen well and share our lives, we can be mutually enriched. Enrichment is the beautiful side of being adaptable.

How can you challenge yourself to be more adaptable?

ABIDING IN HIM

"Abide in Me, and I in you. As the branch cannot bear fruit itself, unless it abides in the vine, neither can you, unless you abide in Me."

JOHN 15:4 NKJV

Jesus was relevant in his teaching. He spoke with shepherds about sheep, wine growers about vineyards, and rulers about authority. What would he say to you to make his message relevant? This Scripture had a dual purpose: it encourages us to remain connected to him, and it requires us to comply with what he asks. Abiding is not just about being coupled to him, but also to act in obedience to him. So Jesus encourages us to remain in him and in hearing his Words, abide by them.

In today's world, all measures of truth are subject to the individual, and our relativistic society disregards the concept of objective truth. This means as followers of Christ and as leaders of others, we bear a burden to remain allied with him and to adhere to the truth which he states. He is abiding with you in your leadership, and you can trust him to guide you in speaking the truth in love.

How does obedience to Christ tie into abiding in him?

Most Talented

He shepherded them according to the integrity of his heart,
And guided them with his skillful hands.

PSALM 78:72 NASB

God is quite the talented being. He made the whole world including humans, and the intricacies and details baffle the mind. People demonstrate skills and abilities that astound many, such as savants, or those with hyperthymesia, or photographic memories. We hear of people who can recount an inordinate number of facts, recall vivid details with a superior memory, or capture book-loads of data in just a few minutes of reading.

There are so many talented individuals, yet somehow people think that God is boring. Why? Is it because he doesn't want us wasting our creative talent on being better at sin? Yes, likely. Our sin actually distracts us from being who he made us to be, creative and fascinated by him. Chasing our fleshly desires is simplistic and dull. Anyone can do that. Utilizing the gifts and talents that he placed within us to accomplish his will is exciting and worshipful.

What can you do to increase your God-given talents?

MOVED BY SONG

Sing to him, sing praise to him;
tell of all his wonderful acts.

1 CHRONICLES 16:9 NIV

If you have ever enjoyed music to the point of being emotional, then you understand what it means to be moved by what you hear. We may not perceive it, but nearly every movie we watch which we consider excellent actually has moving and effective music. In fact, if you watched the same movie without its music, you will probably not have the same reaction to it. It would appear less enticing and would definitely lack emotive quality. Next time you watch a movie take note of what you are feeling and what you are hearing. Mute some of the scenes and you will be engaged mentally, but you will not be moved nearly as much.

Worship that engages music opens our hearts to God. We are moved to connect with him in ways that we do not otherwise. Often Scripture is brought into music because it moved someone at some point in history, and they began to extol God. Something happened which compelled them to sing to him and to make a melody that moved their hearts. Observe in Scripture how many times there is a mention of music, instruments, or singing.

What moves you to worship Jesus?

FOR REAL

Unlike so many, we do not peddle the word of God for profit. On the contrary, in Christ we speak before God with sincerity, as those sent from God.

2 CORINTHIANS 2:17 NIV

It's the look in their eyes. You wonder if they are *for real*. Then you see the look, and hear the voice, and yes, they are sincere. What is it about facial expressions and body language that help us communicate? When it comes to interpersonal communication, only seven percent of what we express is actually through our words. The rest of it is in tone and body language. When it comes to sincerity, humor, anger, or any other emotion, much of what we hear and understand is seen through our eyes and filtered through our experiences.

Sincerity is seen in an honest face with a candid and genuine expression. We imagine Jesus holding out a hand. He is truthful and heartfelt in his love and care for us. There is no trickery or scheming in his eyes. He loves us sincerely.

When you speak to your team, what do they see in your facial expressions and body language as you communicate?

A REAL SACRIFICE

People were bringing little children to Jesus for him to place his hands on them, but the disciples rebuked them. When Jesus saw this, he was indignant. He said to them, "Let the little children come to me, and do not hinder them, for the kingdom of God belongs to such as these."

MARK 10:13-14 NIV

Fostering children takes an enormous amount of work. Time is the first sacrifice. Numerous classes have to be taken to learn how to care for and support hurting children. Those hours could be spent making more money and enjoying life. Also, finances are relinquished in order to foster; new clothing, furniture, toys, and school supplies have to be purchased. Bedding and other items are needed to set up a room or two and to make sure everything passes inspection. The small stipend from the state does not cover it.

But the real sacrifice is likely the disruption in our lives to help with emotional instability in the brokenhearted children. The hearts of foster parents literally ache for these small souls especially when they have to put them back into the homes that first brought the children such pain. This is truly an altruistic service, but it is so worth the sacrifice. Just as Jesus said, God's kingdom is filled with the hearts of children, and serving them is like serving God.

What can you do to inspire volunteer work to help children in your organization?

CENTER OF BLESSING

The LORD your God has blessed you in all the work of your hands. He has watched over your journey through this vast wilderness. These forty years the LORD your God has been with you, and you have not lacked anything.

DEUTERONOMY 2:7 NIV

There are many forms of the word *blessed*. We say, "I have been blessed," meaning that we have favor and fortune in some area of our lives. We hear about the blessed God, which means that he is holy and set apart. We ask God to bless others, which is a prayer of favor and sanctification. And we say, "Blessed be the name of the Lord," which is praise. All of them have one core element—they are centered on God. He is the blessed one and the giver of blessings.

In today's verse, we see how God blesses. He is watching over us throughout our journey. He blesses the work we put our hands to. He is with us always, so we do not lack anything. In our lives, we are blessed.

How is your work and your role at work a blessing in your life?

ASK BOLDLY

"Ask, and it will be given to you; seek, and you will find;
knock, and it will be opened to you."

MATTHEW 7:7 NASB

Coaching a sports team can be stressful. You have to
require practices. You need your team members to run the
same routines and plays, and then they have to watch and
assess during the games as those situations come up. Do
they step up with their new understanding? Do they play
with confidence and impose themselves on the other team?
The most rewarding aspect of coaching is seeing the timid
team members rise up and become leaders. Those who
would never volunteer first come up through the ranks.
By the end of the season, you see them stepping forward.
Similarly as a manager, it is pleasing to see those we have
mentored rise up and successfully complete their work. It is
gratifying to see them present their results like an old-time
pro. It is good to have self-assured, confident people in our
organizations!

The assertive people are in part that way because they have
learned success in being forward with their questions and
the pursuit of knowledge. God encourages us to be like this
with him. Knock, seek, ask, pray, boldly enter, be welcomed,
be hungry…he uses all these words and more in the Word
as he encourages us to come to him.

What do you want from God? Ask boldly!

RELEVANT MESSAGE

"Suppose a woman has ten silver coins and loses one. When
she finds it, she will call in her friends and neighbors and
say, 'Rejoice with me because I have found my lost coin.' In
the same way, there is joy in the presence of God's angels
when even one sinner repents."

LUKE 15:8-10 NLT

The moral of a story is the story-lesson it is trying to teach
us. It is also an ethic, and usually these are tied together.
A lesson teaches ethics. Stories are great at capturing
our attention, and if told well, we can feel them which
helps us to learn from them. Jesus used parables as his
method for teaching morals. Many of them tied directly
to his audience, and they understood them because, more
than just hearing the words, they felt them. Most had
experiences losing sheep or valuables, and plenty had been
invited to a feast.

How would Jesus teach us now? What examples would he
use to make his message relevant to our work environments
so we could understand and learn? God uses our lives to
teach us lessons. Often our workplaces push us, and Jesus
likely has a story to tell us so we can absorb his lesson.

What is God teaching you now?

FAVORITE SPACE

I pray that the God who gives hope will fill you with much
joy and peace while you trust in him.

ROMANS 15:13 NCV

After a hard day's work, especially if it was labor intensive,
what does it feel like to sit down in your favorite chair?
Probably the best. We love to take a load off when we have
been on our feet all day, and the worst way to do that is
to sit on a hard surface. The most comfortable place is
wherever we receive our greatest rest and peace. It's the
place where we can set aside the pressures of management
and still our minds. If we sit down and there is loud music,
screaming children, or animated people, we do not relax. It
needs to be comfortable and peaceful.

This is where God loves to meet us. When we can find a
place of peace and contentment, he is often there waiting.
When we connect with him in this place of ease, we can
hear him more clearly and experience his love for us.

*Where is your place of comfort and how does God connect
with you there?*

GRIT

How long must I wrestle with my thoughts
and day after day have sorrow in my heart?
How long will my enemy triumph over me?

PSALM 13:2 NIV

The man prayed to God, but fear drove him to act in ways that demonstrated his lack of trust. He was busy scheming; he sent ahead gifts of livestock, treasures, and servants. Perhaps his brother would have mercy? Alone, his heart cried out to God, and God met him. He wrestled with God all through the night as his fears and anxieties were driven out and he tenaciously grappled. God said he would bless him, and he would not let go until he received the blessing.

Jacob's determination gave him courage and eventually the blessing came, but with a cost; Jacob limped from that day on. His body was broken, but his spirit was strengthened. He was no longer afraid, and he stepped ahead of his family to meet his brother, confident in the blessing of the Lord. We regularly face fears, difficulties, and stress. Like Jacob, these things weigh heavily on us as we, too, lead others. But God never abandons us. His grit is stronger than our grip, and he will never let us go.

How do you think God handles your anger, fear, or pain?
What do you think God feels when you're fighting with him?

EVERY DETAIL

We are convinced that every detail of our lives is continually woven together for good, for we are his lovers who have been called to fulfill his designed purpose.

ROMANS 8:28 TPT

What keeps you going in life? Is it certainty, creativity, calmness, or chaos? God knew when he created us that mankind would fall. He knew that he was going to have to save us. He had a plan and a purpose for us. His exciting, ultimate goal was to have a people of his own creation who loved him wholeheartedly and who lived with him in his creation. He has given us freewill to choose him and live that love out in a rigorous environment.

This is certain, God will have what he wants. His plan is perfect, and his will for us is included in this end plan. With him we have certainty, creativity, and tranquility which will overcome the chaos. Life is not dull; it is definite. We are not unsure but assured. Our lives are in God's hand.

What keeps you going in life?

DAY OF RESTORATION

According to his promise we are waiting for new heavens
and a new earth in which righteousness dwells.

2 PETER 3:13 ESV

The old boat was haggard. Paint was chipping, some
rowlocks were broken, a few of the floorboards were
cracked, and the hull had a few leaks. The prow was the
worst since it had taken a beating on the rocks over the
years. It was going to be a long and arduous task to rebuild
her. Slowly and methodically, week after week, the builder
worked, starting with the prow, and then moving on. The
final day of restoration came. The old had become new. The
vessel was full of history and ready to write more as she
slipped into the ocean with the crew aboard.

Our vessel is old and haggard. The Shipwright of the
universe will make her right. God will restore the earth and
will raise us up as new creations. The old will be made new!
Our bodies will be restored, and while we will still hold
history, we will be ready to write more.

*What abilities and characteristics do you think you will
retain in the new creation?*

A CLEAR INSTITUTION

Marriage is to be honored by all and the marriage bed kept undefiled, because God will judge sexually immoral and adulterers.

HEBREWS 13:4 CSB

In the beginning, God made marriage a very clear institution of his own design. One man and one woman came together for life; they were separated from their families and joined together to create a new family. Since then, God's people have messed with this design in an effort to make it work with their own selfish desires. People have taken marriage and devalued it, from the kings of Israel to the current generation. God never intended marriage to be treated in the ways it has suffered. It was intended to be held in high regard. To solidify this point, God indicated his intention toward the church as a marriage with himself.

Marriage is a prized and respected entity in God's kingdom. Because he esteems it, so should we. We should celebrate and encourage those marriages around us, as well as our own if we are married.

What can you do to cherish marriage, and how can you encourage it in a society that devalues it?

Open Door

As a father has compassion on his children,
so the Lord has compassion on those who fear him.

PSALM 103:13 NIV

When you buy a beautiful steak, grill it perfectly, and sit down with friends and family to thank Jesus and eat, salvation and salivation come together in one tender moment. It is a beautiful thing when food is cooked such that it melts in your mouth. Eating is a great opportunity for bringing us together, filling bellies, and softening hearts. When we consume food it not only removes our hunger, but it also releases hormones which make us feel good. This physical process actually opens up an emotional and even spiritual doorway to the heart.

Do you have trouble with someone at work? Take them out and eat together. Take time to gently take care of them. Why? God looks for tender hearts because he has a tender heart. He resists the proud because he is not proud. His grace is freely given to the humble. In his family there are people who are compassionate, kind, loving, and gentle. These are the tender attributes of the Spirit of God and you, too, carry them in your heart.

How do you demonstrate tenderness toward others?

GUIDE ROPES

The Sovereign LORD is my strength!
He makes me as surefooted as a deer,
able to tread upon the heights.

HABAKKUK 3:19 NLT

Hiking a mountain is an exhilarating experience even if you are not scaling sheer rock faces. The effort needed for a trek is rewarded by short breaks with beautiful vistas. But there are also uncertain times when footholds are treacherous, and cliffsides are too steep to accomplish without a strenuous climb. Guide ropes may be necessary to help you maneuver around the precipice and to keep your balance. But before you take hold of them, it's wise if you test them. You pull on the rope and make sure it seems firm. Can you trust it to keep you safe?

God gives us his assurance that we can always rely on him. He will not allow us to slip and fall. His promise is to keep us firmly in his grasp and to never let us go. Jesus relied on this security when those around him abandoned him. His friends and family failed him, but he never faltered because God made his steps sure.

If God is for you, who can be against you?

OUR HERITAGE

There is neither Jew nor Greek, there is neither slave nor free, there is no male and female, for you are all one in Christ Jesus.

GALATIANS 3:28 ESV

Paul wrote this word to the church in Galatia who were falling back into Jewish traditions, and, more critically, demanding that people do more for their salvation than what was required. Paul encouraged us to fully believe that it is our faith that makes us God's chosen people, and not our heritage. Earlier in the book of Galatians, he wrote that God does not show favoritism. He does not prefer one person over another even if one of them is Jewish. He loves all people because he is love, and God's love is not exclusive.

Being the embodiment of love means that God does not have it in him to show preferences or favoritism. This does not diminish the importance of God choice of Abraham to establish Israel; it concretes the reason for us to be included as children of God. We express the same faith Abraham exemplified, and this is what makes us one people.

How can you show non-preferential treatment to those around you?

STRENGTH OF MIND

Because the Sovereign LORD helps me,
I will not be disgraced.
Therefore, I have set my face like a stone,
determined to do his will.
And I know that I will not be put to shame.

ISAIAH 50:7 NLT

The young athlete hurt every time she paddled but didn't want the others to know. She was not going to become the focus of the group, and sure didn't want pain interfering with the trip. It was beautiful and peaceful where they were canoeing, and the last thing anyone wants is a whiner. She decided that, despite the pain, she would push through bravely. Carrying a pack hurt too, but through her tough-minded resilience, she willingly carried more than she probably ought to. Of course, this trip had to be the one when the group got lost, so they circled back doing twice the distance with paddling and portaging. Her body took it all because her mind was determined. She showed the backbone and grit of a warrior.

Fortitude is about a strength of mind that does not give way to weaknesses. Jesus demonstrated similar strength of mind and Spirit when he suffered and died for us. He was willing to die for the cause and was resolute in his mind no matter what he suffered.

How does fortitude show up in your life?

ONLY ONE

"No one is holy like the LORD,
For there is none besides You,
Nor is there any rock like our God."

1 SAMUEL 2:2 NKJV

God is holy and ferociously righteous. He cannot tolerate the presence of sin, and any who stand before him in their sin will perish. There is none, no not one, righteous among us. All of us will perish; none of us can stand before God on our own merit because we are all stained with sin. What can we do? Who will save us?

It is Christ, the resurrected Savior, who is righteous! He became a man and walked the earth without any fault. He demonstrated an honorable life and willingly sacrificed his desires to obey God. Then he suffered at our hands and died for us all, blameless and righteous. He bore our sins upon himself so they would not be held against us as we stand before God. His desire is for all mankind to experience this forgiveness and grace and to have a relationship with a holy God. Our choice is to either come to him and follow his ways as we receive his righteousness, or to live our own lives and bear the consequences of our sin before a holy God. There is none besides Jesus Christ.

What helps you choose to claim Christ's righteousness for yourself?

Not Afraid

The LORD is my light and my salvation
so why should I be afraid?
The LORD is my fortress, protecting me from danger,
so why should I tremble?

PSALM 27:1 NLT

Sometimes there are moments when we become troubled by a feeling, but we are not able to identify any threat. We sense that something is wrong, or some impending trouble is coming. This is not a place we like to be for long. Anxiety builds the longer we are in it as we look at our lives and try to forecast each scenario. Am I losing a pivotal employee? Did I forget to file some taxes, or is there a pending financial burden? Are these programs or products going to fail suddenly? It can be overwhelming.

Thank you, Jesus, that you offer a reprieve! The Lord is our light and our salvation. We declare it over all these anxious feelings. We proclaim his protection; we claim his blessing. We trust him fully and if all is taken away, he is our security. Ultimately, we know our lives are promised eternal security and all that we have and do pales in comparison to what he has for us when this life is over. He is our hope; Jesus is how we overcome the pressures of the day.

Today, what gives you confidence despite the troubles you may face?

Extraordinary Willpower

"My food," said Jesus, "is to do the will of him who sent me
and to finish his work. Don't you have a saying, 'It's still four
months until harvest'? I tell you, open your eyes and look at
the fields! They are ripe for harvest."

JOHN 4:34-35 NIV

Within Jesus was a drive to accomplish the Father's will.
He would not relent until he saw what God had completed
whatever was set before him. Jesus understood his role in
his short life on earth, and he fully embraced it. His resolve
to do so allowed him to endure sleepless nights, hunger-
filled days, and immense suffering which led to death.

Did Jesus have any weakness? Yes, he was fully human.
He faced temptation as we did, but he had extraordinary
willpower. He was able to fend off temptation and allow
God to be all that he needed even to the point of not
needing food but relying solely on what God gave him.
He did this as an example for us, not to prove his deity.
He demonstrated, with difficulty and suffering, that we as
humans can live devoted to God's service by his strength.

*Do you have ways that you use willpower to overcome
temptations? Do you find fasting and prayer helpful in your
efforts?*

VALIANT WARRIOR

Put on every piece of God's armor so you will be able to resist the enemy in the time of evil. Then after the battle you will still be standing firm.

EPHESIANS 6:13 NLT

When you think of someone who is valiant, what comes to your mind? You likely think about the brave war hero or the fictional character who beats back a villain. You may be able to picture scenes in your mind and feel the strength they demonstrated as they pushed forth and overcame their adversary.

How many of us think of the person who is on their knees in their room praying and interceding for themselves and others? At first thought it may not seem very bold or brave. But if we truly grasp the spiritual world around us, and we understood the battles occurring in the heavens, we would appreciate that there is great courage in intercession; there is bravery in prayer. There is a need for boldness in order to break down spiritual strongholds—to see the enemy's power broken over homes, cities, and regions. We are prayer warriors empowered with courage from the Holy Spirit. We are the valiant warriors Jesus calls to join him in his war against sin and darkness.

How can you practice valor in prayerful intercession?

QUIET CHARITY

"When you give to someone in need, don't do as the hypocrites do—blowing trumpets in the synagogues and streets to call attention to their acts of charity! I tell you the truth, they have received all the reward they will ever get."

MATTHEW 6:2 NLT

Is it better to give than to receive? When we dwell on this, we may or may not recognize that we have been given so much already. Sometimes we think it would be better to receive, but we have been given so much that our lives should be about giving what we have to others.

What have we been given? Apart from our possessions, we have received forgiveness, salvation, a Christian family, immeasurable grace, kindness, and faithful love. We have the Holy Spirit who fills us and overflows to others, and he marks us for resurrection to an eternal, unblemished inheritance in Christ. This inheritance is everlasting life on a new earth with God dwelling amongst us. No more tears, pain, or sadness. We have enough to give, and in our positions, we are already regularly giving. It doesn't always have to be money, as sometimes that is an easy out, and we have so much more to give of ourselves.

What does it really cost you to give? How can you work on sharing your resources with others?

KEY TO HAPPINESS

Do not be anxious about anything, but in every situation, by prayer and petition, with thanksgiving, present your requests to God.

PHILIPPIANS 4:6 NIV

What is the key to a happy life? If we find happiness, will we be thankful? Surely if we are happy, our hearts will flow with thankfulness? Since the time of Democritus and likely some time before, people have been searching for the definition of happiness. His early philosophy was that happiness was found in the soul, not in possessions. Later philosophers believed it to be found in the balance of pleasure; when happiness abounds over pain, it is dominant.

Christians believe happiness is found in contentment with Christ. When we find contentment, our hearts are in a state of thankfulness. Therefore, Paul wrote that in all things we should be thankful; it is the reason he was content and happy. Let us be mindful to purposefully remain in a place of contentment by continuing to be grateful. We give thanks to God for all of our blessings.

What are you thankful for today? What about your work and those you lead are you thankful for?

LEARNED BEHAVIOR

Teach me to do your will,
for you are my God.
May your gracious Spirit lead me forward
on a firm footing.

PSALM 143:10 NLT

Many people enjoy getting out into nature. Experiencing the good earth that God has created is satisfying to the soul. But sometimes that good turns bad and rages against us. If we are out when a nasty storm hits and the temperature drops suddenly, we can suffer. Our enjoyment turns to regret. It helps if we prepare ahead of time by bringing the necessary equipment so we can remain warm and dry. But this is learned behavior, adopted by either having the experience or listening to those who do.

As volatile as the physical world is, it can also go into the spiritual world. We regularly venture out in it unaware of the dangers. And as we do, it is important to be humble and to listen. There are spiritual repercussions to not following the voice of God's Spirit, and our unprepared situation can get us into trouble. But the Lord is not volatile. He is stable and secure. He is gracious as he sets us on a firm footing. He does not change in his desire to lead us and protect us. Thank God for his angels around us!

How can you be more spiritually aware?

HUNG UP

"Whenever you stand praying, forgive, if you have anything against anyone, so that your Father also who is in heaven may forgive you."

MARK 11:25 ESV

Jesus was hung up on forgiveness. Literally. He made it an imperative in our faith. It isn't optional; it's completely critical to the core of Christianity. How we practice forgiveness is a measure of how we will be forgiven. This is a condemning word because we are fallible, egocentric beings. We demand much of others and little of ourselves. We quarrel and fight because we do not have. When we ask something of God, we do so with the wrong motives.

Before becoming believers, we were friends of the world and enemies of God. Christ came for us, suffered, and died for our sins. He redeemed us and forgave us an insurmountable debt. We could never pay it back. So Jesus asks us to make sure we forgive others as he has forgiven us. *Wow.* If we put that in perspective, how many sins would be mounted against us? Hopefully we choose to embrace the compulsory practice of forgiveness.

When you consider the number of sins Christ has forgiven you of, how does it affect the way you forgive others?

November

Let us not grow weary while doing good, for in due
season we shall reap if we do not lose heart.

GALATIANS 6:9 NKJV

No Compromises

Remember your leaders who have spoken God's word to you. As you carefully observe the outcome of their lives, imitate their faith.

HEBREWS 13:7 CSB

As the manager looked around the table at her team members, she was disturbed to notice a warmer-than-necessary interaction between two of her people. They were sitting too closely, sharing notes, and whispering. Big sigh. Office romances are awkward to handle. After the meeting, she met with the two of them separately. She spoke about mindset, focus, and company goals. She addressed the need for integrity. She asked direct questions and assured them of her discretion. Overall, she pressed for professionalism in their interactions going forward.

Active faith is manifested in the integrity a leader shows in their interactions. When a project is completed, it will stand against the test of time and competition because there were no compromises throughout the process. Righteousness is also a known characteristic that demonstrates a living faith. When office conflicts or difficult relationships arise, a leader can guide and require appropriate behavior to reach a resolution. Parameters for good behavior are high with a believer, but it they can be expected by example and with coaching.

Do you analyze your leadership abilities by looking at the outcomes?

EXCITED IN PEACE

Don't act thoughtlessly, but understand what the Lord
wants you to do.

EPHESIANS 5:17 NLT

When your imagination and your memory come together
to recreate experiences which were full of fun, joy, passion,
thrills, or intensity, what do you picture? It may be a concert,
a sporting event, a person or a group of people, or a holiday.
Sometimes it's all of those. Perhaps you think about a major
accomplishment you achieved at work. We were created to
be at peace but excitable, restful but energetic, content but
pleasure-seeking. These dichotomies are intentional, so our
deeper hunger drives us towards God.

If you have read Psalm 16, you know that we experience all
these variances within our personalities forever. We don't
need to chase after excitement or thoughtlessly take risks.
Right now, God wants a people who are attentive to him,
eager to do his will, *and* excited about their futures in him.
The most satisfying, long-lasting pleasures come when we
encounter the Holy Spirit and follow his lead. Look at the
history of those who have lived fulfilled lives and see how
God moved them to do great things.

*You have the Holy Spirit in you. What exciting thing is he up
to today which you will be doing with him?*

AWE-INSPIRING

When the crowd saw this, they were filled with awe; and they praised God, who had given such authority to man.

MATTHEW 9:8 NIV

If we think humanity is somehow limited, we only need to visit the Great Wall of China to experience an amazing feat of human engineering. The wall is up to eight meters tall and over five meters thick at the top in some sections. It can be seen from the moon!

The worn stone steps to the top of the Wall show where people have trod through the years. As tour groups climb up the wide path, thoughts come to mind of the multitudes over centuries who have climbed them before. How many people have walked this path? How many ethnicities have stepped in this place? It's likely millions have been to the Wall before. And there is no wondering why. At the high points there are incredible views; mountains and valleys with stunning vistas all around. The two perspectives are amazing; a walk along a majestic human achievement and the marvelous awareness that it can be seen from space. Two awe-inspiring moments come together in one beautiful experience. We see the incredible creation God has made and we *are* part of that creation as we gaze around at even more of it.

What do you think your team of God-made beings can accomplish?

STRONGLY PERSUASIVE

I myself am convinced, my brothers and sisters, that you yourselves are full of goodness, filled with knowledge and competent to instruct one another.

ROMANS 15:14 NIV

Some people are strongly persuasive. They exude confidence and clarity of thought which make for sound reasoning. They talk knowledgeably about multiple topics and have thought deeply to come to provoking opinions. There are also people who are persuasive because of their personas. They have a whimsical influence which is charming and warm. They woo others, not just by words but because of their own appeal. We listen to people with specific knowledge that has been thoroughly researched in order to learn more. They are the researchers and teachers of the world.

For what purpose are we to be persuasive except to share Christ with others? Our very purpose is to be knowledgeable about who he is, to be warm like he was, and to teach others as he did. He wants us to demonstrate his love, his mercy, and his kindness.

Does your method of leadership persuade someone to learn more about Jesus?

Pleasant Memories

The LORD is all I need.
He takes care of me.
My share in life has been pleasant;
my part has been beautiful.

PSALM 16:5-6 NCV

We all hope for thoughts like the psalmist's in today's verse when we reflect back on our lives in the end. We pray for pleasant and beautiful memories because the Lord took care of us. What a great way to drop the mic, to walk stage right, to leave planet earth. Are we there now? Can we say now that the Lord is all we need and that he has taken care of those needs? Do we trust him today? And do we look to him for all we have because of that trust?

If our faith in God is firmly entrenched within the fabric of our daily lives, we will be able to say that *our shares* are pleasant and beautiful. Our Father, the Creator, has everything we need to be happy. He doesn't want us focused on what we are producing or how our organizations are functioning to satisfy us. He doesn't even want us lamenting over our failures as some form of artificial motivation to do better. He wants us to look to him and cry out to our Abba Father. He loves to take care of us. This is the only way for rivers of blessings to flow out of our lives to the nations.

Do you have a recent experience that reminds you of how pleasant life in Christ can be?

Enjoying Work

Go to the ant, you sluggard;
consider its ways and be wise!
It has no commander,
no overseer or ruler,
yet it stores its provisions in summer
and gathers its food at harvest.

PROVERBS 6:6-8 NIV

Do you think of the ant as insightful and wise? Perhaps not. It seems they are preprogrammed to do exactly that for which God made them. And that may be the point. God made ants to do certain tasks, and he is telling the lazy man, "I didn't make you for this. Get up now and do the things I made you for!"

God put us to work when he created us. Man named the animals and was a large part of the creation process. We were commissioned to take care of the earth and given rulership over the whole domain. Even after the curse, our work remained even though it was more vigorous; rigorous work does wear us down. However, work is not wrong or evil. It is partially what we are made to do. Balance is important because making it our first priority and shirking it are both ungodly.

What do you enjoy working on the most?

PART OF THE WHOLE

Abandon every display of selfishness.
Possess a greater concern for what matters to others
instead of your own interests.

PHILIPPIANS 2:4 TPT

Humans are independent and like to take care of themselves. It starts from that first cry with a hasty response from our attentive parents, confirming the system. As we grow, we learn that when we do certain things people respond favorably; that is motivation to do them more. This affirmation process develops healthy attachments. If positive efforts are left unchecked, it can also promote self-centeredness. When parents teach their children well, they learn that they are a part of a larger system. As they contribute, the system runs smoothly. All the people within a healthy system are content.

We see this translate into our work environments. Imagine if we could interview potential employees based on family systems and effectively fill our teams with well-discipled workers! What teamwork and productivity could be accomplished then? In the same manner, the body of Christ is best when we work together to share the gospel and also take care of one another. To consider each other in love promotes that love into the communities around us.

How did you learn to be considerate? How can you foster that consideration at work?

SUPPORTIVE

Whoever oppresses a poor man insults his Maker,
but he who is generous to the needy honors him.

PROVERBS 14:31 ESV

Have you ever experienced an injury where you could not walk except with extreme pain? You tried to hobble but ended up collapsing or crawling. Then some caring soul came over, helped you up, and walked alongside you. You were weak and they provided the supportive strength you needed. As humans, we are made to care for all people and all ethnicities. God never intended us to be divided and indifferent.

Jesus declared that we will be known by how we love. Our sacrifices in the effort to support the weak, the broken, and the needy are demonstrated in a real way to the world. It does not matter where people come from. God commands us to support all those in need, and he has given each of us specific gifts to use for philanthropy. We have been endowed with abilities and gifts in leadership, administration, counseling, wisdom, care, finances, and more. We are not limited by skills or resources, although we often lack willingness, a sacrificial desire, and creativity.

What gifts can you use to help those in need?

PRACTICED EXPERTS

I will tell everyone about your righteousness.
All day long I will proclaim your saving power,
though I am not skilled with words.

PSALM 71:15 NLT

Very rarely do we find a person skilled at something
they did not practice. Few are naturally skilled, and for
those who are, likely they had some early developmental
advances, or perhaps even some inherited traits from their
parents. No man can boast in himself because even the
practiced expert probably received his determination and
focus from his parents.

Time and time again we see winners, experts in their fields,
honoring their parents when they talk about their skills.
Sometimes it's because of the way they were raised, and
other times because of inherited traits, but they honor
their parents because they know their mastery was not just
learned by themselves. It is also why many people honor
God. Ultimately the abilities and proficiencies we acquire
come from him. Eventually we recognize that we are made
in his image and for his praises, and not for ours.

*When someone praises you, to what or to whom do you
usually attribute your skills?*

Our Legacy

We will not hide these truths from our children;
we will tell the next generation
about the glorious deeds of the Lord,
about his power and his mighty wonders.

PSALM 78:4 NLT

There is a consistent theme throughout the Bible that gives us great hope—we have an inheritance as God's people. Jesus didn't only redeem us from sin and death, although that is amazing in itself. We have even more to look forward to. Peter wrote that this inheritance is unfading, imperishable, stored in heaven, and waiting for those who believe. What is this legacy? Why do we deserve more than he has already given?

This is the beauty of a heritage: those who are named will receive an inheritance. Is it different for each person? It appears that some slip into heaven, and others are rewarded with big accolades and a larger inheritance. This is similar to what we receive on earth, where all who are named in a will do receive something, but some special items are saved for special relationships. There is a great reward for those who give their lives to Christ and his work first, ahead of or instead of building their own legacy.

What can you pass on to those you work with that will have eternal value?

COMMON THEMES

Wise people can also listen and learn;
even they can find good advice in these words.

PROVERBS 1:5 NCV

Have you ever attended a church where the pastor spoke on
a theme throughout the year? They would present different
messages, but it all led to the same conclusion. You listen to
several hundred messages all built around the same theme
over a few years. It can become monotonous, or you can really
grow in your understanding of that theme. It's your choice.

When you read Proverbs, there are some common themes.
Words are written differently but all point to the same
lesson. One of the most prevalent messages is that the wise
person listens and learns; the fool is not teachable. The fool
is portrayed as headstrong and stubborn, and he remains
bent on doing his own thing. The wise heed instruction;
they listen to wisdom and respond appropriately. Proverbs
is like a themed sermon being taught over and over. Those
who read it and listen will become wise.

What can you do to become more teachable?

HOLISTIC BEINGS

"Nothing is covered up that will not be revealed,
or hidden that will not be known."

LUKE 12:2 ESV

It has been said that to be spiritually mature you must first be emotionally mature. Why? Because our emotional state affects us so deeply. When we are not mature, those things that disturb us quickly diminish our ability to maintain good character. Driving that response is our emotional system, and within it, shame, which hides in layers of behavior, suppositions, and memories.

We must learn to be attuned to our emotions so we can discover what is happening in our brains and our bodies. When we do this, we become healthily aware of our weaknesses, we embrace those things we fear will be exposed, and we allow others to see us for who we are. We become leaders of integrity, spiritually whole, but wholly broken. God is naturally invited into this process as we unfold our lives before him and others. It is a uniquely beautiful and terrifying experience. Indeed, those most vulnerable with their inner lives are the most courageous. We need leaders like that.

What holds you back from being vulnerable with others?

SPIRITUAL STAMINA

What you have learned and received and heard and seen in me—practice these things, and the God of peace will be with you.

PHILIPPIANS 4:9 ESV

What does spiritual stamina look like? Is there a way to build up our spiritual strength so we can endure? Yes, there is. We can do all things through Christ who strengthens us. He gives us stamina. How do we build strength? Paul wrote that God's power is found in our weaknesses; as we recognize and embrace our failure and insufficiency, we find strength in God. We must understand who God is and who we are in light of him. When we humble ourselves, we are strengthened. As we face adversities, we recognize our inability to handle it alone. God uses those times to build our spiritual stamina and our reliance on him.

Spirituality is all about having a relationship with God. Similarly, when people face trouble in a marriage and work through it together, their marital stamina is strengthened. The next round of difficulty is faced with greater endurance. It is no different with God. Our stamina comes from building a healthy, dependent relationship with him.

How do you rely on God when you're being tested?

UNIQUE PURPOSE

From birth I have relied on you;
you brought me forth from my mother's womb.
I will ever praise you.

PSALM 71:6 NIV

Sometimes when we are alone and have nothing to do, our minds drift to thoughts about life and our accomplishments. Does what we do really matter? In this alone space and as we take time to read, who really cares about our existence? Are we just a meaningless task doer? What are we leading others into? If not for what we do, who are we? Is who we are dependent on what we do? Are we vital at all?

The answer to the meaning of life is found in our Creator's Words. He made us and he knows us. He planned us and gave us our unique purpose. He does not wish that any should perish, but that all will come into fellowship with him. His deepest desire is not that we would function perfectly in the realization of our roles, but that we would wholeheartedly embrace our relationships with him. We are essential to our Father, and he loves us for who we are, not what we do.

What does God love about you?

DEEP JOY

Those who look to him for help will be radiant with joy;
no shadow of shame will darken their faces.

PSALM 34:5 NLT

Joy. It's a happy word, short and to the point. Even speaking the word can bring us to laughter. The radiance of joy is as pleasurable in the expression as it is in the experience. Joy gives you strength to dance on the grave of shame and laugh in the face of death.

The joy we receive in Christ is deep. It is much deeper than happiness which is fleeting and likened to a stream that dries up in the heat of summer. Joy remains a strength in the believer that is not easily dampened. It rises and sustains us like a deep spring with an unending source of bubbling water.

How do you sense joy strengthening you in your day-to-day routines?

BE STILL AND WAIT

Be still in the presence of the LORD,
and wait patiently for him to act.
Don't worry about evil people who prosper
or fret about their wicked schemes.

PSALM 37:7 NLT

What does it mean to be still and wait? We would never get anything done if we didn't get moving. Our organizations would fail. Yet the Bible says frequently to wait upon the Lord; to be still and wait. This respite and patience is not about being idle. As we know, the Bible also speaks clearly about the evils of being idle. So, it's not about inactivity but about tranquility.

We can be at peace knowing God will move on our behalf. We don't need to fret or allow ourselves to become anxious. At a practical level, it may mean not signing that deal right away or not letting that employee go. Let God know whatever it is you are anxious to do or to talk about and allow him to be part of your decision-making process. Exercise patience. When people fret and worry which often ends up in sin. Trust in the Lord and allow his Spirit to work in you to give you patience and the ability to be still.

What are you anxious about today that you can invite God to be a part of?

TIME TO PONDER

If anyone is in Christ, he is a new creation.
The old has passed away; behold, the new has come.

2 CORINTHIANS 5:17 ESV

God is magnificent. His splendor is all around us. It does take a moment for us to stop what we are doing and look for it before we notice the wonders around us. This is why God calls us to wait on him, to take time to reflect, and to be still. When we do, we can see his glory and creativity. It causes us to worship him. What he has made is impressive, and we marvel at it.

Even something as simple as a rainy day creates an opportunity to sit and look out the window at the falling rain. We notice and marvel at the single drops that come together, pooling, and swirling. Drops turn into streams and rivers. Lessons through nature become clearer to us. One can only do so much alone; come together with many, and you have energy and power. Single drops join to make a river which quickly turns into a flood. The flood becomes a force to be reckoned with. It's so simple and yet so profound. We just have to take time to ponder.

How does pondering impact your thoughts on your team's projects or on the team members you lead?

A Dollar a Day

"The eyes of the Lord roam throughout the earth, so that
He may strongly support those whose heart is completely
His. You have acted foolishly in this. Indeed, from now on
you will have wars."

2 Chronicles 16:9 nasb

It is easy for many of us to give a dollar a day to support
someone in need. It really is not a big obligation. If we
are not doing this or something similar, we should be
asking ourselves why not. We can also encourage our team
members at work to share with others who live in atrocious
conditions. Can we let go of a latte each week to help a
needy family? Most likely.

We can also invest ourselves and not just finances whether
we're helping a stranger, a missionary, or an overseas effort
to give aid. We can pray for them, care for them, and give
to them. Locally, we can be a comfort, a physical presence,
and a prayer partner. These efforts can be in our work and
in our church communities. It is part of why we are in the
family of God. It is through our love for and support of one
another that the world sees his goodness.

Why do you give to others? If you don't, why not?

GRATITUDE IN SIGHT

Walk in Him, having been firmly rooted and now being built up in Him and established in your faith, just as you were instructed, and overflowing with gratitude.

COLOSSIANS 2:6-7 NASB

If we ever struggle with gratefulness, it is usually because we have lost sight of what blessings we have. We can also become preoccupied with wanting more. Paul wrote that he is thankful at all times. If we ponder this while considering the life that he had, it should stir a sense of wonderment within us. How could he be thankful in all things at all times? He dealt with great suffering and maltreatment. He was beaten, maligned, and disparaged for the sake of Christ, yet he was thankful. How?

Paul kept his eyes on Christ and the hope that he had because he was firmly fixed on Christ's sacrifice and his resurrection. Paul knew that his momentary afflictions were just that—momentary. He didn't need more. His contentment was in knowing that there was a great reward to come. He was confident that Jesus would take care of him in the future.

What is more important: achieving all you can in this life or working to obtain your future inheritance in Christ?

CONDUCTED WITH HONOR

A voice came from heaven:
"You are my Son, whom I love;
with you I am well pleased."

MARK 1:11 NIV

"This man conducted himself with honor." It sounds like a line from a movie, a military story where the skillful leader guided his men through difficulties and trials, and he is being honored for accomplishments. The speakers are filled with pride and a sense of admiration for the honored man.

Jesus heard this same sense of honor from his Father. It is something all of us want to hear from God one day. However, we often feel that our failures are so much more evident than our successes. Remember this: Jesus was just starting his ministry when God spoke these words over him. It was an initiating statement, a declaration. God can do great things through us, directing and guiding us to perform his desires. At the end of it all, he will look at us and say the same words, not because of our deeds but because of his Son, Jesus Christ.

What can you do to earn God's favor, or can you rest in what Christ has completed?

Holy Spirit Wisdom

We continually ask God to fill you with the knowledge of his will through all the wisdom and understanding that the Spirit gives, so that you may live a life worthy of the Lord and please him in every way: bearing fruit in every good work, growing in the knowledge of God.

Colossians 1:9-10 NIV

Where does true wisdom come from? It comes from the Holy Spirit. Worldly wisdom is not a complete waste; it just doesn't please God like the wisdom that comes from his Spirit. Jesus said that God will use foolish things to confound the wise, and the weak things of the world to shame the strong. Why? Because those who are wise and strong do not need God. When we have faith in our own wisdom and strength, eventually we will distance ourselves from him. He knows this. It is why he rejects the proud but gives grace to the humble.

To gain wisdom, true godly wisdom, we need to seek his Spirit. How? We can start by reading the book of Proverbs and substituting the word *wisdom* with *Holy Spirit*. It will give insight.

How can you actively seek wisdom?

A Good Name

A good name is more desirable than great riches;
to be esteemed is better than silver or gold.

PROVERBS 22:1 NIV

Do you know someone with a good name? Perhaps you have a good name. A good name conjures up great favor with people. A reputation goes before a person and makes the way easier like a personal herald. It announces to others that someone of value, honor, and trust is coming. Be ready to heed their instructions and watch their methods; perhaps there is something to learn from them! You may have worked alongside or have been taught by such a person. Perhaps you are lucky enough to still be learning from them! Maybe you are even learning from Jesus.

The person scorned or with a bad reputation stays away because of their shame; they do not want to hear about the esteemed. Honored people walk with their heads held high and are pleased to associate with everyone. They do not have any need or desire to hide with shame or fear. They are respected and esteemed.

Who do you esteem in your life and why?

FROM DARK TO LIGHT

Give thanks for everything to God the Father
in the name of our Lord Jesus Christ.

EPHESIANS 5:20 NLT

Imagine being taken away from your loved ones and your familiar places. Imagine being placed deep within the woods where there is no glimmer of community lights at night, and no moonlight. Now imagine walking around, orienting yourself, and finding a way. But the way to where? Your home? A town? How do you get there without light? You cannot see. Fear becomes your closest friend. You are alone in the dark and unprotected. As fear starts to strangle you and silence overwhelms you, death is nipping at your heels. Suddenly a light cuts through the darkness, and angels surround you. They comfort you and provide you with food and water. The Spirit of God then guides you on a path home, to where you belong.

This is our reality. We were once in darkness, and now we are in the light! We give thanks because, as Paul wrote earlier in this chapter, we were all in darkness, but now we walk to the Father, toward our home. The darkness is still around us, but we are not afraid. There is trouble but we are not overwhelmed. God is our shield and our salvation. In him we trust.

Can you share your gratefulness for salvation in God with someone today?

TOO EASY

Your unfailing love is better than life itself;
how I praise you!
I will praise you as long as I live,
lifting up my hands to you in prayer.
You satisfy me more than the richest feast.
I will praise you with songs of joy.

PSALM 63:3-5 NLT

It is common for us to want things to be easy. For example, we like to not wake up not too early, or to be productive without too much trouble, and we especially like having good relationships without the drama. We want to enjoy life. But some philosophers believe that when life is too easy, we will go looking for trouble. We have an inherent need to be challenged. If life is too sweet, we go looking for lemons.

If we look back at our lives, we may agree. There always seems to be something lacking that we cannot quite put our fingers on. When is life enough? We each have a God-sized hole inside. We are satisfied when we find the place where God meets us. Excitement, peace, ease, and thrill all come together in a satisfying manner. We don't have to wake up too early, we are productive in the best way, and our relationship with God is more than enough.

What is the source of your experiences, both exciting or troublesome, and how can God fill the void?

SHUT IT DOWN

The eyes of the LORD are in every place,
Watching the evil and the good.

PROVERBS 15:3 NASB

The boy pleaded with his father to borrow his iPad. They were traveling, and he wanted to play while they were waiting for their flight to board. The father obliged, knowing that this trip would be dreary without something to do. How could he not? He was reading email on his phone. So the two of them sat a bit of a distance from each other, each on their devices. *Pling*. The dad's face flushed; a woman had propositioned him via messenger. Forgetting that his son had his other device, the father answered. The woman answered back. The father answered again, and it was over.

Years later, the son asked his dad about those messages. As the father remembered the moment, he had no shame at all. They talked about it for a while. What had the father said to the woman that impressed the son? Something good about his wife, no doubt. Integrity is doing the right thing when no one is watching, or when you *think* no one is. You choose honor over shame.

When no one is watching, or you think no one is watching, do you choose righteousness?

Keeping Watch

The Lord sees all we do;
he watches over his friends day and night.
His godly ones receive the answers they seek
whenever they cry out to him.

PSALM 34:15 TPT

In the role of shepherd at your workplace, you realize the importance of safety. You likely see the vulnerabilities of your staff and their work environment. You know it is not just the words they use, but the spirit that operates in and amongst the people. There are also the physical dangers depending on what kind of operation you manage. When you start to consider all these working components, you are aware of your own inability to watch over everything.

Our combined wellbeing of all our working parts is wrapped up in God more than we realize. He sees all that is going on. His invitation to us is to welcome him in and to recognize the concern he has for us. He sees all we do as he watches over us. To God, we are the vulnerable ones—all of us. He wants us to cry out to him in our troubles, or even when we see that we are not enough by ourselves, so he can answer us.

Can you find a place of safety with God where you have peace being with him?

A WITNESS

We cry, "Abba! Father." The Spirit himself testifies with our spirit that we are God's children.

ROMANS 8:15-16 NIV

When you sign a document that needs to be formally submitted, it requires a witness. This is a common requirement throughout legal systems across the globe. It ensures that a signature on a document is not forged, which serves both the signee and the guarantor. We know this in business because every important document relating to ownership, finances, or agreements has a secondary signatory, the witness.

God's promises need no witness, but he makes it clear that the Spirit is a witness that we are his children. We accept the Spirit of God to indwell us as our witness. He is the mark that says we are a child of God. He attests to the fact that we are to be resurrected. God is the guarantor of our resurrection, and the Spirit is the witness who ensures that we are the recipients. It is those who are filled with his Spirit and stand until the end who will be saved.

How does God's Spirit strengthen you to endure each day and to remain full of faith?

EMPTYING YOURSELF

Do nothing out of selfish ambition or vain conceit.
Rather, in humility value others above yourselves.

PHILIPPIANS 2:3 NIV

Paul wrote to inspire the church to love one another
with the exhortation in today's verse. Soon afterward, he
encouraged them to have the same attitude as Christ did;
though Jesus was like God, he did not count himself equal
and emptied himself by becoming a man. In a like manner,
we are to empty ourselves and become like servants to one
another. Can you imagine a group of people living with
the same purpose and love so deeply entrenched in their
behavior that they serve out of ambition for one another?

We see this kind of love, where one lays down everything
for another, in old romance novels. People fell over
themselves to dote on their love interest. We who have been
there but have lost that passion, laugh and tell ourselves
that that was they way it was only in our younger days. But
this is the kind of love that Christ wants us to have for each
other. He wants to see us behave with great affection and
affinity. Out of this place comes a unity of mind, of purpose,
and of spirit. It is here that the Holy Spirit is poured out as
he was in the early days after Jesus' ascension.

*To express value for others, especially for the members of
your team, what would it take for you to set aside your needs
and serve them?*

SHAME CONTROL

Nothing in all creation is hidden from God. Everything is naked and exposed before his eyes, and he is the one to whom we are accountable.

HEBREWS 4:13 NLT

Have you ever watched an animal that has something stuck to it? The classic example is when tape is stuck on their feet. They dance and jump around, trying to get it off. Until they are free from it, they have no ability to focus on anything else. We are like this when it comes to having our vulnerabilities and sins exposed. It is distasteful and foreign to us. Don't look! I don't want you to see my brokenness or my sin. We like to keep control over what we reveal and don't reveal to others. Shame is the driver of this tendency.

Like the animal with tape stuck to its foot, when we feel shame or exposure, we dance around pointing fingers, lying, hiding, and distracting. We'll do anything to avoid being vulnerable. Ironically, God, the true judge, sees right through us. He loves us and wants us to sit still in his presence and like a child, take comfort in him. God is always with us, so why not settle into that deep relationship and accept his love with all vulnerability.

How do you practice vulnerability?

ULTIMATELY VICTORIOUS

I trust in your unfailing love;
my heart rejoices in your salvation.
I will sing the LORD's praise,
for he has been good to me.

PSALM 13:5-6 NIV

We know that Jesus is ultimately victorious. The end will come and when it does, he reigns. But in the meantime, we have to battle this life. We fight the powers of darkness and evil every day. Temptation plagues us. Our minds and emotions are a battleground where our will and action unfold with both success and failure. We work with people and conflicts arise. The tenacious presence of conflict can be overwhelming. We are not always victorious. However, as the psalmist wrote, our perspectives should not be defeatist.

We trust in the unfailing love of God. We know that he is good and continues to be good toward us. We also have a great hope in what is to come: Christ's ultimate victory, the celebration, and the new creation. Our hope is not blinded by day-to-day battles with wins and losses. We keep our eyes fixed on Jesus.

What gives you strength to go another day?

DECEMBER

Know well the condition of your flock,
and pay attention to your herds,
for wealth is not forever;
not even a crown lasts for all time.

Proverbs 27:23-24 CSB

POSITIVE PROGRESS

We are confident of all this because of our great trust
in God through Christ.

2 CORINTHIANS 3:4 NLT

People who are confident are capable of carrying many
burdens in life. Why? Because they perceive those burdens
as weighing less. Those who are confident don't have many
doubts. They believe in what they are doing, they know they
can achieve it, and their focus is given to positive progress.
They effectively work toward improving situations, problem
solving, and hard work. This is the mindset of a leader. They
can carry the load as well as be a strength to others.

Doubts trouble the mind and inhibit effectiveness. It is
God's intention that his people are confident. He wants
his church to trust him to do what is needed. Confidence
and trust are tied together. They work to provide mental,
emotional, and spiritual security which helps to complete
tasks. Doubt and fear attempt to break apart this God-
oriented combination and they only come from one source,
Satan. God is the author of confidence.

*What can you do today to meet the challenge to grow in your
confidence and leadership abilities?*

HEARTFELT EFFORT

We desire each one of you to show the same earnestness to
have the full assurance of hope until the end.

HEBREWS 6:11 ESV

Have you ever had one of those projects where things keep
going wrong? Have you had a season where business is not
great? Sometimes we give our best efforts and things just
don't turn out well. What can we do when this happens?
Hopefully we can find someone to help us, but ultimately it
is God who comforts us and offers the best path forward. He
loves our heartfelt efforts to do things for him and to align
with his purposes. He knows when we earnestly seek his
wisdom and when we sincerely want him to work with us.

We may not always be the best at showing it, but we truly
want God to run things his way but through us as his
effective vessels. Whether in our organizations, or with the
people we serve, or in our homes, we want God leading us.
Our hope is in him.

*What do you suppose God thinks of your efforts? Are they
ultimately for him or for you?*

TRULY WELCOMED

> "I was hungry and you gave me something to eat;
> I was thirsty and you gave me something to drink;
> I was a stranger and you took me in."
>
> MATTHEW 25:35 CSB

In some cultures, being welcomed can be an overwhelming process. If you have ever been formally welcomed by some tribal cultures, it can be a loud, emotive experience. After an initial dance, notable chiefs get up-close and personal by pressing noses and foreheads together with the visitors. The experience of a tribal welcome almost makes you feel that you are a part of the tribe.

The point of truly welcoming someone is to make them feel at home and part of the family. Hospitality is big on God's list of Christian attributes. He even makes it a priority in determining who is fit to lead the church. Throughout the Old and New Testaments, God made it clear that we are to receive the stranger, care for the needy, and to be up-close and personal by sharing our lives with them. We do this so that, ultimately, they can meet the Father.

When a new employee starts work with your team, how can you make them feel welcome?

A Different Place

Teach me your way, O Lord,
that I may walk in your truth;
unite my heart to fear your name.

PSALM 86:11 ESV

God's truth is eternal. It is sensible and reasoned; it is not divided. The cry of the psalmist in today's verse was to hear and know God's way. He wanted his heart to be complete in revering the Lord. How do we learn from God? How conscious are we of what he speaks to us? Do we listen to the Holy Spirit in our day-to-day lives? His Spirit is truth and speaks truth to us if we have the ears to hear. When we ask to walk in truth, we are really saying we want to walk in the Holy Spirit.

Imagine people walking in the Spirit everywhere. This would mean being surrounded by people who were honest, loving, kind, considerate, patient, and full of joy. The world would be a different place. It would be heavenly; it's what God intends for us in the future. When we are aware of the Holy Spirit, and we allow his voice to become familiar to us, we will be changed. We will learn what it means to walk in the truth and to wholeheartedly serve him.

How can you practice awareness of the Holy Spirit?

DON'T DO

From days of old they have not heard or perceived by ear,
Nor has the eye seen a God besides You,
Who acts in behalf of one who waits for Him.

ISAIAH 64:4 NASB

"Ok, God. This one is not going to move on its own. I have to do something." Have you ever been in that spot with a looming deadline and nothing but your own efforts to depend on? We face trials all the time when it seems that if we don't do something, nothing will change. That decisive, action-oriented strength is what every leader needs. Despite that strength, however, there are times when we cannot move that mountain, and it takes God's intervention to get it to shift. Our role then is to pause, to rest in him, and to wait. That is not easy.

It takes an immense amount of discipline to *not* do something. But be assured of this: when we surrender these mountains to God and wait upon him, we can fully depend upon his Spirit, and he will show up. The move may not look like what we originally anticipated, but he will be faithful, and he will act on your behalf. Wait upon him and the result will be beautiful. He is faithful.

Recall how God has moved mountains in the past when you could not. What did you do to ask for God's help? What did you do when you saw the result?

A Strong Follower

"Anyone who wants to serve me must follow me, because my servants must be where I am. And the Father will honor anyone who serves me."

JOHN 12:26 NLT

The mighty men of valor are specifically honored in the Old Testament. The Hebrew word for valor is *chayil* and it means, "to talk about men under strong leadership who performed mighty deeds protecting their families and loved ones." The word is wonderfully descriptive for the true warriors who were good at following orders and accomplishing their leaders' assigned tasks.

The best leaders are found among these kinds of people. You may have been plucked from many because of your ability to be a strong follower. It is a foundational element for being a good leader. In fact, God honors the servant as possessing the highest of all qualities; we see this in Christ, our servant King. He laid down everything to lead us into victory. God raised him up and honored him above all.

What can you do today that would compel God to honor you when you stand before him?

PARDONED

Let the wicked one abandon his way,
and the sinful one his thoughts;
let him return to the LORD,
so he may have compassion on him,
and to our God, for he will freely forgive.

ISAIAH 55:7 CSB

For anyone standing trial and facing judgment, what sweet relief it would be to hear the words, "Not guilty." But if you were guilty, what would it feel like if the judge told you that you are pardoned because another man is paying for your sentence? *Flabbergasted* might seem like an appropriate word. How incredible would it be to receive a pardon and walk away having no penalty to pay because someone else has paid it? All the sweat, tears, and remorse we felt as we stood before the judge would be gone. Our responses would vacillate between relief, reflection, and exuberant celebration.

This is how we should live every day. We have every reason to spend our lives in utter amazement that, despite our state of depravity and our continuous sinful state, we have been forgiven our debts. We have been acquitted and released from death. What an amazing God we serve! His compassions are innumerous. His faithfulness is astounding.

How would you respond if all your sins were on display in court, and yet the judge let you go free?

GIFT OF AWARENESS

In all your ways submit to him,
and he will make your paths straight.

PROVERBS 3:6 NIV

The ability to perceive a developing situation and to shrewdly prepare for it is a gift. Those who are insightful are able to use their awareness to see oncoming dangers. When this gift of awareness is submitted to God's Spirit, it can be helpful in relationships, and it is wonderfully useful in prayer. Counselors are often gifted with understanding and discernment which is why they are helpful in seeing troubling situations and then speaking into them. But when this gift is self-serving and not used for God's purposes or no longer other-focused, it can become manipulative.

As with all gifts, perception is given to many people for the specific purpose of serving and loving each other. We must learn to take each gift that God has given us and submitting them to him. When they are used to love him and to love others, we know our gifts are serving the right purposes.

What strengths do you see in yourself? How are they being used for God?

STAY SEPARATE

Flee youthful passions and pursue righteousness, faith, love, and peace, along with those who call on the Lord from a pure heart.

2 TIMOTHY 2:22 ESV

Do we still have passions and impure desires even though we are maturing in our salvation? Yes, we do. Regardless of age, the enemy continues to tempt every one of us. It does not matter what our positions or places are in life, we are still subject to the desire of the eyes, the lust of the flesh, and the pride of life.

But when we are young, our prefrontal cortex has not fully developed yet. We may act on impulsive decisions. For this reason, the more mature Christians need to encourage the younger ones to hungrily chase after God. Paul told us that whether we are young or old, we need to call on the Lord. We need to cry out to him, and he will be there. If we are in pursuit of God, it will bring about our transformation. When we get ahold of Christ, we are naturally determined to keep him. In truth, he actually keeps us, but the best way for us to remain in him is in our efforts to stay separate from the world and free from the love of what it offers.

How are you able to remain unwavering in the face of your temptations?

START OF LOVE

Above all, maintain constant love for one another,
since love covers a multitude of sins.

1 PETER 4:8 CSB

Love started with Jesus. He loved us so much that he
left heaven and came to earth. God himself became a
dependent baby, suffered immensely, and died a horrible
death, all to cover our sins with his love and righteousness.
But he didn't stop there. Jesus continues still to pray for us,
and he extends forgiveness to us each day. He covers us
with his justice, mercy, and love. Wow. Let that sink in.

How must we act when we consider this constant love?
How do we present the Spirit to the people we work with?
He asks us to consistently love each other enough that it
will cover the hurts that we dole out to each other. How
often do we gripe about little things people do which we
find intolerable? Jesus encourages us to let those things go
and to have grace as he does. He wants us to let go of the
complaints and to stop harboring hurt. As he does for us
each day, he asks us to do for others.

How can you be more gracious to others each day?

FEELING CONNECTED

"I am the sprouting vine and you're my branches.
As you live in union with me as your source, fruitfulness
will stream from within you—but when you live
separated from me you are powerless."

JOHN 15:5 TPT

Christmas is a great season for feeling connected, especially when you start the Christmas decorating. That arduous work of hanging lights, checking bulbs, connecting wires, covering trees, and trimming hearth and home has to be completed before you can enjoy it. But it is fun to do the decorations together. The real satisfaction comes when you connect everything and turn it on. Once the strings of bulbs are connected to the power, everything lights up and that brings great joy. There's a sense of satisfaction with what has been created. It doesn't seem to get old, either. You can have the same setup for years and there is always a wonderful pleasure in seeing everything in its place.

Connecting with God is similar. Things light up in our lives even when you're the same old person you've dealt with for years. And each time we reconnect with God, there are similar emotions which bring a sense of joy and pleasure.

How does the Holy Spirit bring you into closer connection with God?

RECEIVING GIFTS

All of this is for your benefit. And as God's grace reaches more and more people, there will be great thanksgiving, and God will receive more and more glory.

2 CORINTHIANS 4:15 NLT

Christmas rolls around every year, and we are excited to participate in the giving and receiving of gifts. It is an especially exciting time for children. When there are many gifts to be received, a child can be so excited about opening them that they don't take time to acknowledge what they were given. They quickly lay aside one gift so they can get on to opening the next one. When they open that one particular gift they were wanting, there is a great, pleasurable response. They may even keep going back to it between the opening of the other gifts. That gift was well received.

Much like our faith, when we don't take time to acknowledge what we have been given, but we just take ungraciously, our hearts can lose the delight in recognizing what Christ gives to us each day. When we take time to enjoy his gifts and open our hearts to go back to visit them regularly, we receive his gifts well.

How can you ensure that God's gifts are well received in your life?

SPIRIT OF TRUTH

"The Spirit of truth. The world cannot accept him,
because it neither sees him nor knows him.
But you know him, for he lives with you and will be in you."

JOHN 14:17 NIV

The Bible is clear that deceit will be common in the final days of this world. Jesus encourages us to not be deceived but to be alert. He wants us to watch carefully and to not be caught up in the hype of this age. We have been given a treasure to protect in the Spirit of truth. He is with us always, bringing to light the deceit of men, of ourselves, and of the evil one. The more we mature in our faith, the more we recognize the need for his truth. We become spiritually sharpened and more sensitive to his voice.

This is how we will know when Jesus returns: his Spirit will confirm the truth and the timing with our spirit. But we also should be careful not to be alone in this. We are to remain in the body of Christ, so we do not become deceived ourselves. The Spirit of Christ operates within the context of the church, not apart from it. We find truth in the body of Christ which is confirmed by the Spirit of truth.

How often are you in relationships with people of faith?

THOUGHTFUL CARE

If anyone sees a fellow believer in need and has the means to help him, yet shows no pity and closes his heart against him, how is it even possible that God's love lives in him?

1 JOHN 3:17 TPT

Compassion is a strength in believers that blesses people in need. It enables a hurting person to be heard and understood when they freely express what they feel. When we are understood, we can begin the process of healing. This is an important aspect of our relationships inside and outside of the workplace. We know this ourselves because Jesus is compassionate. He connects with us on all levels, and he grasps what we are experiencing.

God feels what we feel. His tenderness to us is evident when we are broken or in pain. Experiencing the compassion and comfort he brings gives us the ability to express thoughtful care for others. We can comfort those who are suffering because he comforted us. In this way his love is demonstrated in us.

Who needs your compassion right now?

REAL LIVE SAINT

Keeping our eyes on Jesus, the pioneer and perfecter of our faith. For the joy that lay before him, he endured the cross, despising the shame, and sat down at the right hand of the throne of God.

HEBREWS 12:2 CSB

There was a good man once, and his mannerisms led everyone who met him believe that a real live saint walked the earth. He spoke with gentleness. Wisdom came from his lips like water flowing over a waterfall. Like honey is sweet to taste and good for the body, so his words were a delight to hear and good for pondering. He practiced patience with all and served anyone who came to him for help. He was a willing soul. Could you lay fault at his feet? Not unless you knew of some deep, dark secret, and he had none.

He lived until he was ninety-eight years old, and because of his unwavering faith in Jesus and his discipline to live according to God's instructions, he was content to live or die. His life was devoted to God either way. He was a man who walked humbly with God and lived his life as an example to all.

What testimony are you leaving for others?

TRIUMPHANT

Thank God! He gives us victory over sin and death through our Lord Jesus Christ.

1 CORINTHIANS 15:57 NLT

Do we know what it means to truly be a victor? We are not bloodied in our workplaces in the true sense of battle, but we do experience victories when we overcome obstacles and achieve audacious goals. But the battle is triumphant because there are glorious people of valor. They understand the thrill of victory and the sacrifices required to have that victory. True victors have paid a great cost. They know what it means to lay down their lives for a cause and to win. That is real triumph.

Jesus is the final victor. He shares the spoils with us, knowing that we, too, have overcome and sacrificed to do so. Even so, the glory and the spoils go to him. We are his riches, his inheritance, his bride. He is our wealth, along with the new heaven, and the new earth, and eternity with him. Thank you, Jesus, for all you give us in your triumph!

How does Jesus' victory over sin and death impact your life?

What You Inherit

Everything created by God is good, and nothing is to be rejected if it is received with gratitude.

1 Timothy 4:4 nasb

What are you going to receive from the generation before you? Have you ever thought about it? Do you have a mentor or a previous manager who advises your work? You are inheriting wisdom, advice, and insights from them. Perhaps in your family you will inherit very little, or maybe you will receive a great deal more than you thought. We may think of inheritance as what we will receive upon the death of the people from a previous generation, but inheritance is also an active and ongoing quality. We are receiving their traits, habits, and wisdom now.

God has already granted us so much that we sometimes fail to recognize the good traits and habits in ourselves. How can we be wise about what we do with them? We must rely on the Spirit to develop us into the people he desires so that God can do the good things he has planned with the inherited qualities we have been given.

What are you doing with the inheritance you have been given?

SOVEREIGN LOVE

Yahweh, you are my soul's celebration.
How could I ever forget the miracles of kindness
you've done for me?

PSALM 103:2 TPT

It is interesting to think that God existed as three: Father, Son, and Holy Spirit, before time began. Why would an autonomous being, self-existing and everlasting, desire to bring messy humans into their relationship? Did he need someone to rule over or was he bored? When we begin to study the nature of God and his characteristics, it becomes clear. As a lover, he wants to share more of his love. He is not looking for someone to push around, and he does not want to punish anyone. It's his deepest desire that each person seeks a relationship with him.

God's sovereignty is supreme but not for the purpose of lording it over his creation. It is for enjoyment; he takes delight in what he has made. This is the beauty of the God we serve. Although he holds the utmost power and dominance, he gives it away and shares it with his creation.

How does God demonstrate his sovereign love to you?

FAILURE AND RESTORATION

"Today the LORD has proclaimed to you to be His special people, just as He promised you, that you should keep all His commandments."

DEUTERONOMY 26:18 NKJV

Israel was chosen by God to be an example to the nations around them. He gave them land, blessed them in many other ways, and promised that if they followed his law, they would dwell with him securely in their midst for eternity. They failed miserably, and he gave them over to the nations around them. Since Old Testament times they have been an example of both mankind's failure and God's restoration. God knew that they would fail, but he had a plan of redemption which would be brought about through Jesus Christ. He used the law to demonstrate our wickedness; our hearts are given over to sin forever unless we follow God's redemptive plan. He used grace through Christ and the repentance of our sinful hearts to give us eternal life.

Our hearts need healing before we can follow God's Spirit. Through Christ, he healed us and wrote the law on our hearts. He filled us with his Spirit, and now even those of us who are Gentiles can enjoy being chosen by him. By his Spirit we are all grafted in and confirmed as God's chosen people.

What does it feel like to be adopted and chosen by God to be a part of his family?

LEAST OF ALL

God has proved his love by giving us his greatest treasure, the gift of his Son. And since God freely offered him up as the sacrifice for us all, he certainly won't withhold from us anything else he has to give.

ROMANS 8:32 TPT

Jesus was born in a manger in the town of Bethlehem, with animals and shepherds around him. The Creator became human and was born into poverty. He was surrounded by shepherds and their animals and without any riches or glory. The greatest gift to humanity began his earthly life as the least of all, and he lived his life to serve them. He spent his time mostly with outcasts and people of low status.

We have been given an extravagant gift. We have within us the same Spirit that was in Christ Jesus. The resurrection power of Christ lives in us! He is the assurance of our salvation and the mark that makes us his. Every believer is given the Holy Spirit and the gifts of God's perfect plan to use in service to God and others, especially to those in need.

What can you use your gifts for, and how can they serve those in need at work and in the world?

MAKE IT A REALITY

Faith is the assurance of things hoped for,
the conviction of things not seen.

HEBREWS 11:1 ESV

Most of us had a dream of making something of ourselves as we were growing up. Back in the day, it was popular to want to be a fireman or nurse. We wanted to be heroes. Did we have a conviction about it? Was it really tested? Likely not. We could be convinced to become a doctor to save lives, or we would perhaps think about being a pilot or an astronaut. Even a heavy machinery operator was a solid replacement. But our assurance that we were going to do these things was not based on anything more than a temporary infatuation. Very few of us made it a reality.

Assurance of faith is not based on infatuation. It is based on the confidence and conviction that Jesus is who he says he is. Jesus offers this security because he demonstrated it in his role as the only true hero. He paid the ultimate cost to save all our lives, and this assures us of our salvation and resurrection.

You may not be a hero like Jesus, but how can you help your team have confidence in their leaders?

MOST SIGNIFICANT

The LORD said to Samuel, "Don't look at how handsome
Eliab is or how tall he is, because I have not chosen him.
God does not see the same way people see. People look at
the outside of a person, but the LORD looks at the heart."

1 SAMUEL 16:7 NCV

David took care of the sheep as a boy, and he did it well.
He would watch as the lambs frolicked in the fields and
the ewes ate nearby them. The ram would lay watching
and chewing, always chewing. He was a fat king in his own
mind, but he was relaxed because the boy did his work well.
David took care of large predators and saved his flock many
times. He was small in stature and not much to look at, but
he was brave hearted, and he worshiped his God above all.
This is what the prophet, Samuel, found when he looked for
a future king to anoint. It wasn't Eliab, the tall, handsome
firstborn. God told Samuel to take the last, smallest, most
insignificant son to be presented to him. This was the one
most like a servant and who tended the sheep while such an
important guest visited.

God does not choose us based on human standards. He
doesn't look for what we think is best. He chooses the weak,
the broken, and the needy. He chose us and not on our
merit but because he is love.

*When you see those you serve, do you recognize both the
humble stature and the grand performer?*

Key to Sufficiency

> "You must not covet your neighbor's house. You must not covet your neighbor's wife, male or female servant, ox or donkey, or anything else that belongs to your neighbor."
>
> Exodus 20:17 NLT

The enemy of contentment is comparison. It is hard not to compare when you see that sweet ride drive by, a luxurious home, or that stunning spouse: none are ours, but we want them anyway because of comparison. If most of us were thankful for what we had, what we had would be enough. Thankfulness is the key to sufficiency.

When we dive into comparison, we covet. Then we attempt to find replacements for the things we are discontented with. We need to turn to God and tell him how we feel and what we want, not so that he gives us those things—he is not Santa Claus. But he does listen, and he wants to speak to us. He wants us to understand that all he has given us is adequate. He wants to turn our hearts to him and away from any distractions. When we communicate with God, he turns our hearts and our eyes back to him. What we have is sufficient and we only need to look to him.

What are you trying to replace that you already have and can be thankful for?

In Light of Eternity

Our light affliction, which is but for a moment, is working
for us a far more exceeding and eternal weight of glory.

2 Corinthians 4:17 nkjv

When we read Scripture, it appears that those who walk
in righteous ways will not be harmed. They will live long
and flourish. Contrast that assumption with the psalmist's
writings about his frustration with the success of the
wicked! God seems to turn away his eyes from their
evil ways and allow them all liberties and wild success.
They ravage the weak, displace the poor, and cheat their
adversaries. Why do they prosper? How am I to live a
long, healthy, peaceful existence when these evil men run
rampant throughout the land?

God does promise us good things. He does guarantee our
health, wealth, and life. Just like the disciples who were
confused about the timing of his kingdom, we can be
confused too. He has promised excellent things in light of
eternity where we will have all of these commitments and
more. In this life, we will have trouble, but he is our comfort.

In your affliction, who or what do you look to for comfort?

INCREDIBLE WONDER

An angel of the Lord appeared to them, and the glory of the
Lord shone around them… "I bring you good news that
will cause great joy for all the people. Today in the town of
David a Savior has been born to you; he is the Messiah,
the Lord."

LUKE 2:9-11 NIV

The incarnation of Jesus Christ is an incredible wonder to
dwell upon. What an amazing way to demonstrate love.
Who gives up ruling with authority and power and takes
every risk imaginable to become like those he created?
Compare the wealthiest most powerful person on the
planet. Would they revert to infancy, suffer, and die to save
others? No. We are too selfish to do that.

Jesus did not come down and become a king. He did not
arrive on a throne or to a kingdom. He became a babe.
He was completely dependent on imperfect parents who
started their marriage in a questionable way, at least from
a human perspective. Then he became a prince? No, he
became a carpenter like his human father. When he started
his ministry, he traveled and depended on others for food
and shelter. He lived simply and held no title. His life
was played out with humble steps which lead to suffering
and shame as he hung on a cross. His incarnation is a
marvelously selfless act of incredible love.

*What events in the life of Christ make you wonder about
God's decisions?*

MAKE HIM PROUD

The precepts of the LORD are right,
giving joy to the heart.
The commands of the LORD are radiant,
giving light to the eyes.

PSALM 19:8 NIV

It is a pleasure when we are set on a righteous path or commissioned to a task, and we conquer the challenge that we set out to do. There is satisfaction in completing a job, pride in what was accomplished, and honored by the commissioners. It is right and good to experience these things and to enjoy them. God made us to work and also to enjoy it. It was only after the curse that it became difficult. Despite the curse, God continues to give us work to do, to walk in his ways, and to follow his commands. When we do these things and we crush it, we feel great!

How awesome it is to do the Lord's will and to make him proud! He is a good Father, and like all good fathers, he enjoys it when his children obey him. We are also proud when our team completes their objectives. Sometimes we take them for granted, assuming that their reward is a paycheck. But it's better if we encourage their productivity by expressing our enthusiasm for their achievements.

How can you help your team enjoy their wins?

CHRISTIAN AMBITION

We make it our goal to please him,
whether we are at home in the body or away from it.

2 CORINTHIANS 5:9 NIV

Why do we call ourselves Christians? Is it because we want eternal security, or because we need something outside of ourselves to make sense of the world? Perhaps it is because we want to have a relationship with God and know him like he knows us. Hopefully it's all of the above. Christian ambition, the drive to be successful in our faith, should be this: to know God, to love him, and to demonstrate that love to others. Our ambition should serve as a testimony to who God is in our lives. It should bring others to want to know him. How this looks in your work environment is between you and the Lord. He will have a plan for how you can show his love to those you lead. In drawing close to him, he will reveal it.

We cannot make Christianity a profession where we look right, do good things, and practice a religion. Our faith is much more than that because it is based on a relationship and knowing that person in the relationship. Faith is not a list of tasks or a to-do list. This is why we strive to make Christ known. Through our relationships with God, we're praying that many others will also want to have that intimate relationship with him.

What is your ambition in Christ?

WORTHY OF EXULTATION

"Give praise to the LORD, proclaim his name;
make known among the nations what he has done,
and proclaim that his name is exalted.
Sing to the LORD, for he has done glorious things;
let this be known to all the world."

ISAIAH 12:4-5 NIV

What is truly worthy of exultation in our lives? We love to promote great things we have done or wonderful things we have made. Perhaps we boast about our education, our job, or our many acquaintances. Or maybe we lift up others in our lives who have done great things.

Whatever we do or whomever we glorify, are they actually more worthy of our praise than God? No! Maybe we are not really thinking about who he is and what he has done for us. Our praises and our boasts must be in him alone. We will make known to the nations the praises and practices of our God. He has done glorious things that we will exclaim to everyone. Yes, sometimes we would rather not embarrass ourselves by boasting about him. However, he says that despite our weaknesses, he will make us strong. His grace gives us the opportunities to proclaim his name.

How do others hear of your faith in Christ?

LOYAL THROUGH ALL

"Though He slay me,
yet will I trust Him."

JOB 13:15 NKJV

There is great security in a loyal relationship. When things get difficult loyalty strives to be steady. It does not deny the right to be upset or to ponder a scenario. A person should weigh every situation and be wise, but loyalty provides a strength in partnership that overcomes adversity. It is focused on what two or more can accomplish together instead of going it alone.

Loyalty demonstrates allegiance that goes beyond troubles, hurts, or pain. It says, "I will be with you in this. I will fight with you. Though you slay me, I will give you my trust." That devotion comes from complete trust in God. We know man will fail, but God is faithful. If we rest in his promises of resurrection, justice, and paradise, we can let go of pain and hurt in order to remain steadfast.

Though it may cost you in all your relationships, as it
pertains to God, are you willing to demonstrate loyalty?

FASCINATING KINGDOM

Be in awe before his majesty.
Be in awe before such power and might!
Come worship wonderful Yahweh,
arrayed in all his splendor,
bowing in worship as he appears in the beauty of holiness.
Give him the honor due his name.

PSALM 29:2 TPT

When you plan your actions in detail, or you know what you will do after work, or you have anticipated each step to accomplish a task, the process becomes part of the fascination. You are captivated by what you want to do. Perhaps you are going to clear the trees on a property or paint them on a canvas. Maybe you're writing a song or creating a video. Whatever has taken your imagination and your interest is likely a passion that is worthy of your time and thought life. This is when we know we are fascinated by something.

Jesus longs for us to be fascinated by the things of his kingdom. He wants us to go deeply into the treasures that he has stored up for us. If we listen carefully, he tells us that all these wonderful things that we pursue on earth are but a glimpse of what he has in store for us later. Make Jesus and his kingdom your fascination this coming year.

What fascinates you about God's kingdom?

CONSECRATE YOURSELF

You are a chosen people, royal priests, a holy nation, a
people for God's own possession. You were chosen to tell
about the wonderful acts of God, who called you out of
darkness into his wonderful light.

1 PETER 2:9 NCV

God has chosen us. We don't know how, and we don't know
why. We may want to know because it would perhaps give
us more understanding about ourselves or our worth. But
in reality, it is not about us or that he chose us specifically.
It is about God. He is holy, wonderful, merciful, and great.
That is why we are to tell others about him.

We were set apart not because of ourselves, but because
he consecrated us based on who he is. He calls us to act
accordingly: to be holy because he is holy. We continue
each day to set ourselves apart from the world even though
we are in it. We strive not to love the world but to devote
our hearts to God. As we wrap up this year, let's challenge
ourselves to start the next one with hearts fervent in pursuit
of Christ.

How can you consecrate yourself to God in the New Year?